Pots & Plants

Design and Make the Pot
Grow and Shape the Plant
for Total Artistic Pleasure

Pots & Plants

*

Raymond Bridwell & Roger Churches

* Author of the Best Selling Hydroponic Gardening

Photography by Neal Stevens

Published by
Woodbridge Press Publishing Company
Santa Barbara, California 93111

Published by

Woodbridge Press Publishing Company
Post Office Box 6189
Santa Barbara, California 93111

Copyright © 1977 by Raymond Bridwell and Roger Churches

Library of Congress Catalog Card Number: 76-13772

International Standard Book Number: 0-912800-32-1

Published simultaneously in the United States and Canada

Printed in the United States of America

Dedication

To Hazel Bridwell and Sharon Churches

Contents

Preface: **Two Master Teachers** 9

Introduction by Raymond Bridwell:
  The Joining of Pot and Plant 11

Introduction by Roger Churches:
  Your Individuality in Clay and Plants 15

Part 1:
Supplies and Basic Information About Pottery
  Introduction 23
  Work Space 23
  Sources of Ceramic Supplies 25
  Tools and Equipment 27
  Kilns 29
  Clay 31
  Glazes 35

Part 2:
Planter Projects
    Introduction 41
    List of Planter Projects 42
    Preparing Clay: Wedging and Kneading 44
    Pots & Plants—The Projects:
        Paddle and Scoop Planter with Cacti
           and Succulents 51
        Pinch Planter with Herbs 55
        Petal Planter with False Aralia 61
        Coil Planter with Asparagus Fern 67
        Hanging Coil Planter with Piggyback 77
        Slab Box Planter with Cobra-Leaf Plectranthus 91
        Modular Planter with Palm 111
        Spherical Mold Planter with Swedish Ivy
           and Wandering Jew 121
        Lamp Planter (Core Mold) with Asparagus Fern
           and Wandering Jew 141
        Double Planter (Drape Mold) with
           Crinkle-Leaf Peperomia 153
    How To Use a Kiln 160
    How To Mix and Apply Glazes 166

Part 3
Houseplant Care
    Supplies 173
    Special Potting Instructions 175
    Hints on Pruning 192

Part 4
Appendix
    Ceramic Suppliers 200
    Table of Kiln Temperatures 202
    Glaze Formulas 203
    Glossary of Ceramic Terms 204
    Glossary of House Plant Terms 207

Preface

Two Master Teachers

This book presents two master teachers to share their inspiration and skills with you. A master artist and craftsman, Roger Churches, gives you insights and instruction for conceiving and forming truly individualized plant containers that perfectly complement your favorite plants. A master horticulturalist, Raymond Bridwell, shares his lifetime of experience in selecting and culturing plants perfectly attuned to the artistic qualities of your containers.

Perfect unity, perfect artistic harmony between container and plant—a total creation of rewarding grace and beauty: that is what this book is about.

Raymond Bridwell is the author of the best selling book **Hydroponic Gardening,** the No. 1 book in its field. He is an outstanding consultant on horticultural and agricultural matters, an experienced nurseryman, and a specialist in horticultural anthropology.

Roger Churches is chairman of the department of fine arts, Loma Linda University in Southern California, and a master of the ceramic arts. His students have come from the ends of the earth and now they include you!

Your experience with these master teachers in creating the projects in this book and in learning artistic principles involved in bringing pot and plant together will be enriching and rewarding.

—The Publishers

Introduction by Raymond Bridwell;

The Joining of Pot and Plant

One of the most frequent questions I hear from people who grow houseplants is—Where can I find interesting and individualized pots for my plants? Many plant lovers would like to exhibit their favorites in other than traditional or commercial containers. I've tried to encourage people to make their own pots from wood and other materials, but there is a great longing to be able to create in ceramics.

The expense of the potter's wheel has held many people back from making ceramic pots. But Roger Churches, the co-author of this book, opened a whole new world for me when he showed me how to make clay pottery without a wheel. I was so impressed by the beautiful pots he created that I decided to make a six-state tour of dealers in pots and plants. I think we will now be seeing more pot dealers stocking clay supplies for people who want to create their own pots.

We should approach the joining of pot and plant with as much thought and care as any other artistic endeavor. But

how are we to know, other than by trial and error, what plant will suit what pot and vice versa?

The main principles to remember in suiting pot to plant are harmony and practicality. You want a pot whose size, shape, texture, design and color will harmonize with those same qualities in the plant. Yet you also want a pot that will be practical, that will be appropriate for the growing needs of the plant. For instance, a plant may need a lot of space for its roots or it may prefer a shallow area; a plant may need to be hung, or it may be set on a table.

How do we determine what will bring about harmony between plant and pot? Sometimes harmony will result from similarity between plant and pot. Certain colors in a plant's leaves for example, may be repeated in the colors of the glaze (glassy coating) used on a pot. The shape of a leaf may be imitated in the shape of the designs worked into the clay. The slenderness of stalk and foliage of a plant may be emphasized gracefully by a pot with a tall and slim shape.

On the other hand, a desirable contrast may be created by the differences between the pot and plant. A pot with a textured surface may offer an interesting contrast to a plant with smooth leaves. A very "busy" looking plant may compete with a highly decorated pot, and so a simpler pot may show off both to their best advantage.

The idea is to strike a balance between the pot and plant so that neither will be neglected at first or second glance. After all, if your plant overshadows your pot, why spend all that time creating a special pot for it? And if your pot dazzles but your plant looks like an afterthought, why not just display your pot as a piece of ceramic art without any plant at all?

Another consideration to keep in mind is the living, changing nature of a plant. A plant will grow, and you have to project what your plant will look like in a few months— whether its leaves will completely overhang the pot's sides and cover them from view; whether the plant will grow so tall that it will outsize its pot quickly; whether there will be flowers in the spring that will add a color effect which will enhance the color and design of the pot.

Ultimately, it will be your artistic sensitivity that will guide your decision to bring a certain plant together with a certain pot—your sense of taste, your appreciation for nature, and your own personality.

Making your own pots is going to be an experience in artistic creation. As a plant owner, you already have a great love for the grace, beauty, power and delicacy of plants. You are familiar with the intriguing silhouettes the shapes, the intricate branchings that make indoor plant growing so rewarding. And you have a hand in helping to shape that beauty through proper planting, pruning, watering and feeding.

Now you are about to enter a new dimension, the shaping of the container in which your plants will live—creating an artistic unity that is pleasurable and rewarding.

Of course, you don't have to start with a plant first and make a pot for it. You can begin with one of the planter styles that Roger presents in this book, and then browse through the nursery until you discover the perfect inhabitant for your pot. This encourages you to consider all sorts of plants that ordinarily you might pass by—because you will be looking at colors and forms of plants in a new, deeper way.

Once you have your pot and your plant, the first thing to do is to pot the plant correctly, to give it a proper home. I have written sections discussing potting supplies, potting techniques and pruning, starting on p. 175. I illustrate how to make a special device I use for pots that have no drainage holes (since some of Roger's pots are made without them), called the Bridwell Sleeve. There is also a glossary of planting terms in the Appendix.

I would like to thank Roger, an artist and craftsman who has given me, and I hope you too, an entirely new way to enjoy plants. He has shown us how to shape a form out of clay that is both aesthetic and practical, coordinating pot and plant.

How To Express Yourself with Clay & Plants

Putting together pots and plants can be a beautiful experience. Ceramic pots, made of clay as they are, have a natural harmony with the plants that grow in them. Soil and leaf and sun are like the earth, fire and water that form the clay pot—basic unrefined elements of nature.

Many potters work almost exclusively on the potter's wheel. However, people potentially interested in working with clay often have the misconception that pottery making can only be done in this manner. The wheel is a very useful tool. But the wheel does limit the shapes you can make, and it requires many hours of practice before the neophyte can begin to be rewarded for his efforts.

The beginning potter who is making pottery without the wheel can see results quickly, using the methods of handbuilding described in this book. All of these projects can be done in your kitchen. The basic tools are very inexpensive, and the cost of all materials for one pot plus the

15

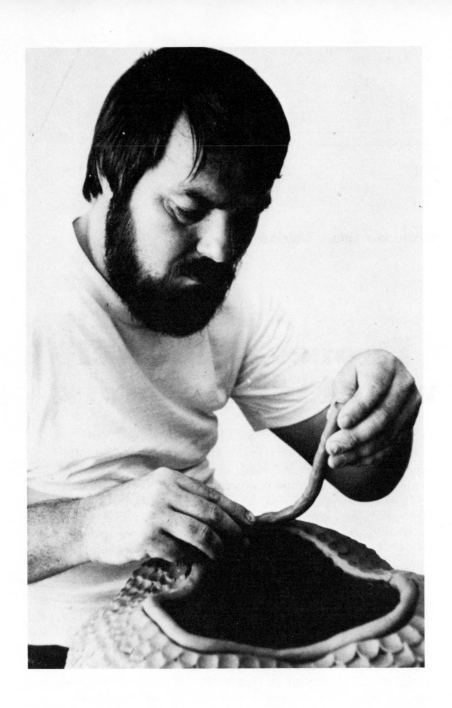

cost of firing the pot in a kiln (a special oven) should be less than a dinner in a moderately priced restaurant.

The skills required for handbuilding are varied, yet not very difficult. In the beginning of your handbuilding experience, not all your work is likely to be successful. But then, there is a degree of risk in any learning process. Mistakes will inevitably be made before we can better understand ourselves and the potential of the material we are exploring. With practice and close attention to instructions, however, failure will be limited.

The projects in this book are arranged in order of increasing difficulty. When followed in succession, they will give the beginner both an understanding of technique and an understanding of the artistic possibilities of the clay medium.

My advice to the beginner is to start with the first project. Read the instructions and look carefully over each photograph. After you understand what is happening, begin and build a pot technically similar to the one illustrated, following the sequences step-by-step. By imitation, you will develop your skills, and gain confidence in your abilities to tackle each succeeding project.

Clay is a unique material, behaving differently than wax, stone, wood or metal. It is an exciting and responsive material to work with, readily taking the form you give it. However, you can push it too far. With practice you will discover its limits and become responsive to them, and you will also discover its potential to embody the flights of your imagination.

After a while you will begin to visualize new ideas for your own variations of the kinds of pots I present here. Nature is a source of many of my ideas for pottery shapes and textures. I particularly enjoy finding beautiful pebbles shaped by the forces of the surf or the currents of a river. Each finely shaped pebble tells a different story of origin, and recorded on it are the results of the slow, deliberate workings of the elements.

Another continuing inspiration to me is plant life. Seed pods hold their precious germ, exploding in spring to spill out their fertile contents. Somehow these seed pods are very much like the clay that holds the potential of a shape, which it unfolds under your hands and gives out to the world.

Textures of the bark of a tree, the pattern of delicate leaves, or the shape of fragile young plants as they force their way through the ancient soil are all models for what you can create yourself with clay. The houseplant for which you make a pot will be perhaps the best stimulus for your imagination. Often the profile of the plant is the most important consideration in fitting a pot to a plant. The color, shape and texture of the plant may suggest to you what sort of pot to make.

In my own work, my intent is not to copy a natural object in clay but to allow nature to be a point of departure in the art of pottery-making. I believe that if the potter is in harmony with nature and the creator, he can develop an intuitive sense of rightness in his work. If you are open to your surroundings ideas will come to you faster than you can bring them to form.

Man since his beginning has been fascinated with clay and its potential to serve him. As a potter, he has ritually formed beautiful vessels and made them hard, strong and durable with the magic of his fire. He works with the elements of the earth, acting as the catalyst that brings them together. He puts function and meaning into his vessels and sculptures as he takes that shapeless mass of clay and forms it into something of value to be later used and perhaps treasured by generations. The history of ceramics extends from the primitive technology of campfire-made pottery to the sophistication of ceramic materials used in the space industry.

Working with clay can serve a new function in today's society. A human need exists to be more in control of our surroundings. As much as industrialization has contributed to our physical well-being, we have in the process become more or less alienated from nature and from other human beings. We have the need to establish a lifestyle that is human and natural, and we can begin to do that by bringing objects that express these qualities into our environment. Better yet, we can be directly involved with a process that will bring us even closer to an understanding of human and natural values. Working with your own two hands with clay, bringing into form a vessel to hold your beautiful growing plants, is surely an enrichment of our lives.

It seems that I have strayed a bit in my discussion of the practical problems of how to make pots using this book as a guide, to more ethereal ideas. But perhaps I have shared with you insights that may help you to become a more sensitive potter. Hopefully you are now eager to make unique pots to hold your plants.

The first part of the book will describe what supplies and tools you will need, and some basics of working with clay. The second part contains a full explanation of each planter project. In the Appendix there is a listing of ceramic suppliers, a few formulas I use to make my own glazes, a chart of kiln temperatures, and a glossary of ceramic terms.

So let's get started on our adventure!

Part 1

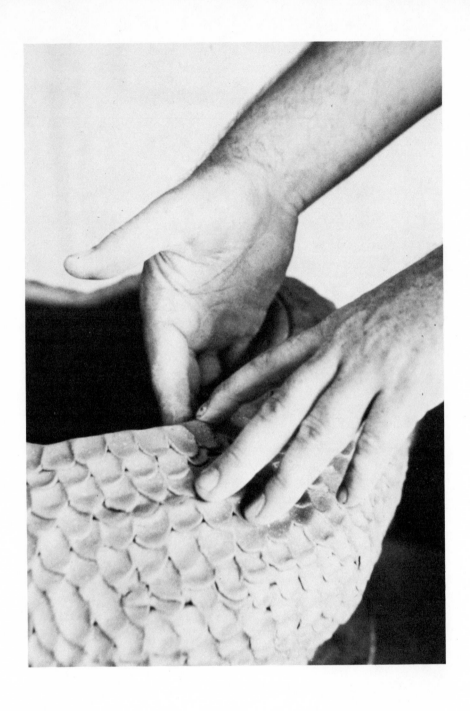

Part 1

Supplies & Basic Information about Pottery

Introduction

Before you start on your first planter, you will need to set up a good work space, and obtain the correct tools and ceramic supplies. This section will guide you in these preliminary steps.

The order of topics will be:
1. Work Space
2. Sources of Ceramic Supplies
3. Tools and Equipment
4. Kilns
5. Clays
6. Glazes

WORK SPACE

All projects in this book may be done in the kitchen. However, you will feel much more comfortable working in a space specially prepared for ceramics. This need not be elaborate and expensive, and can be the same place used for planting in the finished pots.

The following are the primary considerations in planning a work area.

A Source of Water

You need a readily accessible source of water. If you use a sink, precautions should be taken to prevent clay and plaster from going down the drain and stopping up your lines. Use a preliminary wash bucket to avoid this problem.

A Work Table

Your table should be sturdy, and at a comfortable height for working. If you use your table for wedging clay in addition to shaping the clay into pots (wedging is the process of preparing the clay for use, described on p. 45), I advise a wedging surface that will allow you to work at the height of your fingertips when you are standing with your arms hanging down at your sides.

The work table should be a minimum of several square feet in area. The more space, the easier it will be to organize your work

Storage Space

You will need a place to store your tools, supplies and planters in progress. Clay needs to be kept in a container that is not exposed to the air, so that the clay will not dry out quickly. I use an old refrigerator placed on its back, with the latch removed from the door so that it opens like the lid to a chest. The refrigerator is air-tight and works very well for this purpose, but you may use any air-tight box or ccntainer. It should be large enough to hold a standard 25-lb. block of clay.

You will also need a place to keep your unfinished pots that are in the process of being shaped or are waiting to dry and be fired. "Ware boards" are used for this — wood, masonite or boards of any other material that can be stacked up with bricks like shelves.

You don't need much room as a beginning potter. However, the more involved you become with making pots

for your plants, the more storage space you will require
you may also want to store your plant potting supplies (soil
mixes, plant foods, etc.) in the same area.

A Receptacle for Scrap Clay

All of your scraps of clay should be collected, instead of
being thrown away. I put my scraps into a large plastic
trash barrel with water, and every so often take out the clay
and dry it on flat slabs of plaster. The plaster absorbs
the excess water out of the clay and dries it to a
working consistency within several hours. If you are not
doing much pottery work, you can use a container smaller
than a trash barrel to collect your scraps.

SOURCES OF CERAMIC SUPPLIES

Before beginning your exploration of plant pottery, you
will need special tools and supplies. You probably will not
have to look far for them.

First, ask your local high school and college art
departments and professional potters in the community
where they obtain their ceramic supplies. Locate the best
local resources to save yourself time and money.

Sometimes art supply stores and building suppliers carry
pottery-making supplies.

After checking these local sources, you may find that you
need materials not available in your immediate area. A list
of major suppliers is available in the Appendix, on p. 200.
You may wish to contact one close to you, and ask for a
catalog and price list. Most catalogs will provide
descriptions of clay and glazes, and I don't know of any
ceramic supplier who does not handle mail orders.

Your ceramic supplier can be a very helpful person. He
usually knows his materials well and often has had
experience as a potter. He should be able to advise you on
selecting clays and glazes suitable for your planters.

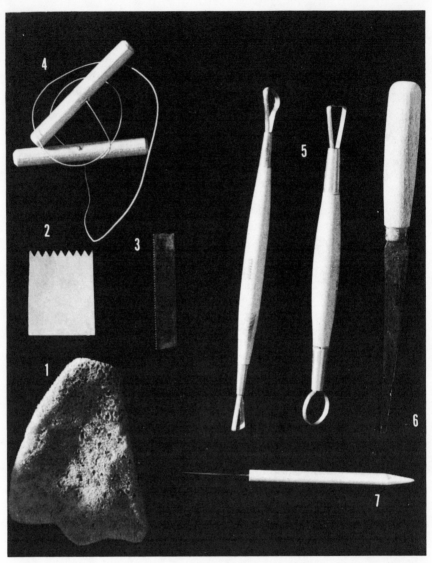

Numbers refer to list on opposite page.

The total investment in pottery supplies will not be very high, since the tools, clay and glazes are all relatively inexpensive.

TOOLS AND EQUIPMENT

For handbuilding with clay you do not need many tools. The ones you see here will probably serve you well for all the projects in this book, and are quite inexpensive. If you need other tools, you can improvise with whatever you have available.

You should obtain the following basic tools before beginning:

1. **Natural sponge** — choose one from 2″ to 4″ across; a natural sponge is more flexible, softer, and easier to work with clay than a cellulose sponge.

2. **Toothed blade or fork** — used for texturing clay and as an aid in joining together slabs of clay.

3. **Piece of hacksaw blade** — for making textures and scraping off rough spots in the clay.

4. **Cutting wire** — usually a twisted wire with handles on each end, used in cutting clay.

5. **Wire loop tools** — for textures and design work.

6. **Fettling knife** — for cutting shapes and many other uses.

7. **Needle tool** — for piercing, cutting and other uses.

For certain of the planters in this book, you will also need the following (they can be obtained as you come to each project):

Burlap or Canvas — on which to roll out clay for making slabs.

Casting plaster — bought in dry powder form from a building supplier; used for making molds.

Paddle — a wooden stick a few inches across but thin-edged, used to tap clay into shape; makes textures.

Plastic sheet — such as a dry cleaning bag or a painter's dropcloth; used to keep the pot from drying out too much as you work on it.

Sticks — at least two sticks ⅜" thick and 18-24 inches long, used to guide the cutting of ⅜" thick slabs of clay.

Wedging and Kneading Board

You need a hard, porous surface for wedging and kneading clay (the process of preparing clay for use by working out the air bubbles and getting it to an even consistency). I prefer to work on a plaster slab. You can make one by nailing together a wood frame and pouring a mix of plaster into it (see the plaster mixing instructions in this book, in sequence J-1 — J-3, p. 124). The plaster slab must be thick enough to withstand hard pounding. I use a slab 2½" thick and 18" square. The plaster slab must be completely dry before it can be used.

You can also use an unfinished wood plank for wedging and kneading.

Banding Wheel (Optional)

You may wish to purchase a banding wheel to hold your pot as you work. There are many brands sold by different suppliers. However, they are all very similar in function. Essentially, a banding wheel is a turntable mounted on a stand, like a lazy Susan. It enables you to place your pot on a surface that can be rotated to any desired position. It is convenient in helping you to work on all sides of your pot easily, but it is not necessary for these planter projects.

You may also use the banding wheel as an aid in decorating your pottery. You can spin the wheel around as you apply bands of color with a brush — hence its name, banding wheel.

KILNS

A kiln is a special oven-like chamber for gradually heating and then gradually cooling your pottery so that it hardens permanently after you have shaped it into its final form. This process is called firing.

Locate a kiln that you can use before you start on your first project. Many people gain access to kilns by taking adult education classes in ceramics through their local school district. Often high school art departments, community college and university art departments, and recreation centers will have kilns that you can use. You can also ask your ceramic supply store for the locations of kilns in your community, or look under Ceramics in the Yellow Pages.

A common procedure is to buy or rent "kiln space " — that is, you pay a modest fee to have your pots fired. Rates may be determined in one of several ways—by the piece, by weight, by cubic inches of space used, etc. The cost should be fairly reasonable.

Since many pieces of pottery can be fired at the same time in one kiln, you may have to wait until a full load of pottery is accumulated for a firing. When firing your ware with others, you will find it interesting to talk to other people working in ceramics. You can exchange ideas and get a chance to see some of the techniques that other students and professionals are using — the more inspiration, the better!

When you arrange for access to a kiln, find out what kind it is. Kilns may be classified as low-temperature or high-temperature. This information will help you determine what kind of clay to purchase, because some clay can only be fired at low temperatures and other clays need a higher temperature (see the following section on Clay).

Note that you will be using the kiln twice for each planter that you make. The first firing will harden the clay into the shape you desire. The second firing is done after you apply a coating of glass, called a glaze, on the pot. The first firing can take about 24 hours, and the second firing can take a couple of days (this includes the time it takes to heat up the pottery and to cool it down slowly).

Consult the section on How to Use a Kiln (p. 160), for details of how to fire your planters. You will also find information there on what to look for if you are thinking of buying your own kiln.

CLAY

There are three types of clay you can use for handbuilding planters: earthenware, stoneware, and porcelain. Your choice will depend on the type of kiln you are using (whether low or high-temperature), and the kind of pot you want to make.

Earthenware clay is the only type of clay that can be fired in a low-temperature kiln. It is also possible to fire earthenware in a high-temperature kiln provided the heat is turned off so it does not increase beyond the maturation (hardening) temperature of earthenware clay.

Earthenware clay is very plastic, that is, it is easy to shape into various forms.

Planters made from earthenware clay are usually a brick-red color, which is the result of iron in the clay. Red clay flowerpots are a familiar commercial earthenware product. Earthenware can also be grey, white or light brown.

An advantage of earthenware is its ability to be vividly colored with the application of a glaze (a glassy coating you can put over the fired pot). Glazes used on earthenware clay include a full spectrum of bright colors. Many of these colorants would burn out at the high temperatures used for other kinds of clay. You will be able to choose from a range of brilliant glaze colors to make containers that will be striking in color and a beautiful contrast to the lower-key hues of your plants. Glazes can also be used sparingly, for example as bands of color on a natural earthenware background, to highlight the colors of foliage and blossoms.

Earthenware glazes come in different textures. Gloss is frequently used; however, other semi-gloss and mat-flat surfaces are possible.

Stoneware Clay

Stoneware clay can only be fired in a high-temperature kiln. It is a very suitable clay for the handbuilt planters

described in this book. In fact, all of the pots illustrated here are made with stoneware clay — it is my personal preference because I like the way it feels and responds. However, you can use other types of clay for these projects if you wish.

Stoneware clay ranges in color from light buff to a dark iron red or dark brown.

Glazes for stoneware pottery are more limited in color than earthenware glazes. Although you forfeit the range of color possible when you use stoneware, you gain a subtlety of color and texture reminiscent of the colors and textures found in nature. Stoneware glazes are muted and rich in tone. They help to achieve a quiet, natural harmony with the soil and foliage of your plants, suggestive of the passage of time and the working of natural processes. Such glazes can create a special mood or setting for your plants — like that of the deep earth, the distant ocean, the soft hymn of the breeze.

Porcelain Clay

Porcelain clay requires very high heat to bring about maturity (fusing and proper hardening) in the pot you are firing and so porcelain must be fired in a high-temperature kiln.

The pottery made from porcelain is usually fine and delicate and can be very elegant. It is white or off-white when fired.

Porcelain clay is not, however, a suitable material for the beginner to use. It is not very easily worked, and requires a great deal of patience and practice.

General Characteristics of Clay

It is my desire to have you obtain clay that will give you every possible advantage in helping you to handbuild your planters successfully. Foremost is the need to buy properly prepared clay that will handle well as you shape and fire it.

The best place to get a good, predictable clay is from your ceramic supply dealer. He can help you in your selection.

The clay you buy can be either dry or moist. I recommend moist clay, because it is difficult for beginners to judge how much water to mix with the dry powder. The supplier has already added the proper amount of water to the moist clay that you purchase. After you become familiar with clay and know how it should respond, you may wish to mix your own clay from powder to save money.

Moist clay is usually available in 25 lb. blocks. You will be able to make two or three or more of the planters shown in this book from one block of clay. A block of clay is quite low in price. Some stores sell smaller 4-6 lb. blocks suitable for a small project.

Whatever kind of clay your purchase — whether earthenware or stoneware — it will have to be specially prepared to minimize warping and cracking problems which are more likely to occur in handbuilt pottery than in forms made on the potter's wheel. A filler can be added to the clay before you buy it to decrease the likelihood of one of these problems occurring Fillers are made of sand or "grog" (a clay which has been fired, ground, and then screened to various mesh sizes).

I use about 15-20 percent filler (by volume) in my stoneware clay. Check with your supplier to make sure that the right amount of filler is present in the clay that you purchase. You can tell if your clay does not have the right proportion of filler in it when you work with it. A clay with too much filler is not very flexible, and will easily crack while you are shaping it. A clay with too little filler will result in your pottery cracking and warping during drying and firing. If either of these happen, talk to your supplier about getting a clay which is more suitable for handbuilding. Or you can add your own extra filler, if needed, at home (the process is described in the section on Wedging, p. 45).

An advanced potter may at some point find it interesting and useful to study the geology and chemistry of clays. However, this is not essential for learning how to make your planter projects.

GLAZES

The glaze is the "icing on the cake," the glassy coating that can make your planter shimmer with gentle hues or shine in a burst of color. By combining several glazes you can give almost limitless expression to your imagination, blending and mixing colors.

Glazes also make possible a range of surfaces, from glossy and smooth to flat (mat). This will enhance the texture of the clay beneath it.

As well as adding color and texture, glazes also serve two practical functions: they seal the clay from moisture, and make your pottery easier to clean.

In buying glazes, be sure that you purchase the types appropriate to the kind of clay you are using (whether earthenware or stoneware). Check with your supplier to see that your glaze and your clay can be fired at the same temperature, because you will be firing your pot with the glaze on it as well as beforehand.

Avoid glazes which contain lead since lead can be toxic to plants and people.

You can buy prepared glaze from your ceramic supplier, or you can make your own glaze. At this point you should explore the possibilities of color combinations and develop your skill with clay rather than concentrate on making glazes. Therefore, I recommend that you purchase a prepared glaze. For the more advanced potter, I have included in the Appendix some formulas I have used successfully to mix my own glazes (p. 203).

Prepared glazes come in two forms: as a dry mix, or already mixed to the proper liquid consistency. I suggest the dry mix because it is less expensive, and not difficult to mix.

Most glazes will keep well in a covered container for an indefinite period of time. Some glazes contain soluble materials which will dissipate. Others will settle out and become hard when not used. Ask your supplier which glazes will keep well after being mixed.

How much glaze should you buy? I prefer to have on hand about a gallon of each type glaze I want to use. However, you don't actually apply anywhere near this amount of glaze for a single pot. Many times I have used only one cup of glaze to cover a small pot.

How many different glazes should you buy? To start, you need not have many different colors. With two or three glazes you can get a surprising number of color combinations and effects. You can put one glaze over another to create a new color (e.g. blue on yellow to make green). One glaze over another can also create a new texture. You can obtain different effects by applying a glaze thickly or thinly. The same glaze will look different on a textured pot than on a smooth one.

When choosing glaze colors, keep in mind the general hues of the plants you will be potting. Foliage is generally a shade of green, combined often with red, brown and/or white. Some plants also have shades of yellow, violet, orange and blue, and of course flowers can be of any color. You want your glaze colors to relate to your plant's colors, to complement or harmonize with them.

You will find most of your glazing needs met with a limited number of glaze colors. I prefer a white, a dark brown, and one or two other colors.

To give you even more possible variations with just a few glazes, use stains (which you can purchase separately) painted over a glaze. Stains are also technically known as metallic oxides. Examples of stains are iron (for browns), cobalt (for blue), and copper (for red and green). Stains are easy to apply after mixing with water, using a brush.

See the section starting on p. 166, How To Mix and Apply Glazes, for instructions on how to use glazes.

The glaze is applied to the pot after you have already fired it once in a kiln. Then the glazed pot will require a second firing. Consult the section on p. 160, How To Use a Kiln, for details of the glaze firing.

As you develop your interest in making pots for plants, you may want to find out more about glaze materials. An excellent text for this purpose is **Clay and Glazes for the Potter** by Daniel Rhodes, published by Chilton Book Co. (Philadelphia), 1973.

Part 2

Part 2

Planter Projects

Introduction

Now that you have obtained your supplies and have a place to work, you are ready to begin an exploration into the creative art of making pottery for your plants.

Each planter is presented as a complete project that you can do, starting from the raw clay and ending with the "perfect plant" in the "perfect" finished pot! The specific plants shown in the photographs are presented as examples, so that you can see what will make a good match to a particular style of pot. They were chosen because you should be able to find these or similar varieties of plants almost anywhere. But I encourage you to consider all of your favorite plants as possible subjects. As you learn to experiment with different planter shapes, sizes, colors of glazes and textures, you will be able to adapt these basic pottery styles to fit every variety of plant in your indoor garden.

The first thing you must do for every project is to prepare your clay properly. The process is called wedging and kneading, and it is the first technique illustrated.

Over a dozen planter projects follow. They are arranged to begin with the simple and move on to more complex techniques. The demonstrations are illustrated very thoroughly and are accompanied by step-by-step instructions. All of the projects use the basic method of handbuilding.

The first three projects will give you a feeling for the clay and beginners are advised to start with these before attempting the later, more difficult pieces. You will find that even the simpler techniques will result in beautiful planters, and these pots are particularly well suited for certain kinds of plants.

As you bring more experience to your clay, and begin to learn the art of handbuilding, you will see many possible variations on the forms illustrated. I encourage you to explore a technique carefully, following each instruction, and produce a pot in the manner you see here. Then using the same technique or a variation of it, create a pot that is uniquely your own design.

Keep in mind that after shaping a pot, you will have to let it dry thoroughly and fire it in a kiln so that it hardens permanently. If you wish to glaze the pot, the glazing must be done after this first kiln firing. Then fire the pot a second time to bake the glaze onto the clay. Consult the sections beginning on p. 160 for information on applying glazes and use of the kiln.

Your finished pot is now ready for planting. In Part III of this book, starting on p. 171, you will find that Raymond has written special sections on potting supplies and methods of potting plants. He also discusses how to prune your plants to keep them looking healthy, well-groomed and attractive.

List of Planter Projects

The planter projects in this book are listed by name. The first part of the name refers to the pottery technique used.

The second part of the name describes what kind of plant is used in the example shown.

After each project name and a picture of the finished planter, you will find a commentary by both authors on why the pot design was chosen for this plant, and vice versa. Then there will be a general description of the pottery technique used, and illustrated directions for making the pot. Sometimes you will find a separate sequence first, showing a special technique used in making a type of planter, before you are given instructions for the specific planter itself.

Following the planter instructions you will often be shown variations on that pottery style, to give you an idea of the range of possibilities you can try. In addition, you may be directed to sections in Part III of the book on how to pot or prune the plant used in that particular project.

Planter Projects

1. Paddle and Scoop Planter with Cacti and Succulents   51
2. Pinch Planter with Herbs   55
3. Petal Planter with False Aralia   61
4. Coil Planter with Asparagus Fern   67
     Coil Technique   68
     Making Coils   69
     Coil Planter   71
5. Hanging Coil Planter with Piggyback   77
     Coil Textures   78
     Hanging Coil Planter   84
     Variation: Textured Coil Planter with Spider Plant   89
6. Slab Box Planter with Cobra-Leaf Plectranthus   91
     Slab Technique   92
     Stamping Textures in Slab Walls   93
     Variation: Curved Slab Box Planter with Crassula
          Tetragona   109
7. Modular Planter with Palm   111

8. Spherical Mold Planter with Swedish Ivy
   and Wandering Jew   121
       Molds   122
       Making a Plaster Hemisphere Mold   123
       Spherical Mold Planter   129
       Variation 1: Hanging Hemisphere Planter with
                   Plectranthus Africanus   135
       Variation 2: High-Footed Bowl Planter with
                   Spider Plant   136
       Variation 3: Open Coil Planter with Melon
                   Peperomia   139
       Variation 4: Woven Bowl Planter   137
9. Lamp Planter (Core Mold) with Asparagus Fern
   and Wandering Jew   141
       Variation: Tall Cylinders with Wandering Jew
10. Double Planter (Drape Mold) with Crinkle-Leaf
   Peperomia   153

PREPARING CLAY: WEDGING AND KNEADING

Before you can begin shaping a pot with your clay, it must be free of air pockets and of an even consistency, Otherwise the clay pot may crack when you fire it, since air trapped inside the clay will expand when heated.

You can eliminate air spaces and make your clay smooth and homogenous throughout by a process called wedging and kneading. This is somewhat similar to kneading dough.

You will need a hard, porous surface to work on, one that will not allow the clay to stick. You can use an unfinished wood plank or a plaster slab. If you wish, you can make your own plaster wedging slab by following the directions on p. 28. If you use a plaster slab, avoid getting plaster chips in your clay; it will cause your pot to break in the firing.

You can use either the wedging technique or the kneading technique as shown to prepare your clay, or a combination of the two. Wedging is the easiest for beginners, but it is a considerably slower process than kneading. The following illustration will demonstrate both methods.

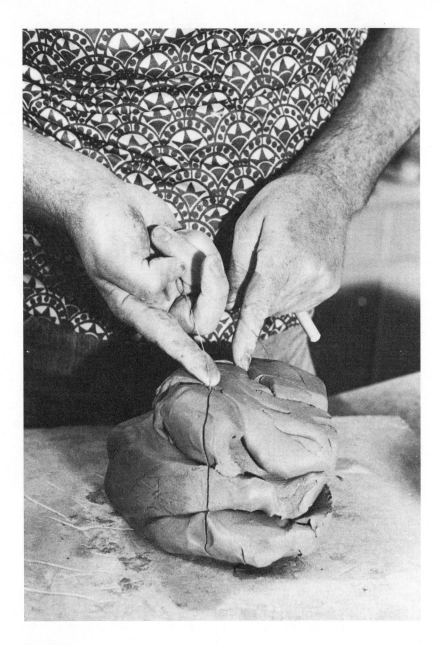

Wedging

Wedging 1. Cut a large mass of clay into two pieces as shown here, using a cutting wire.

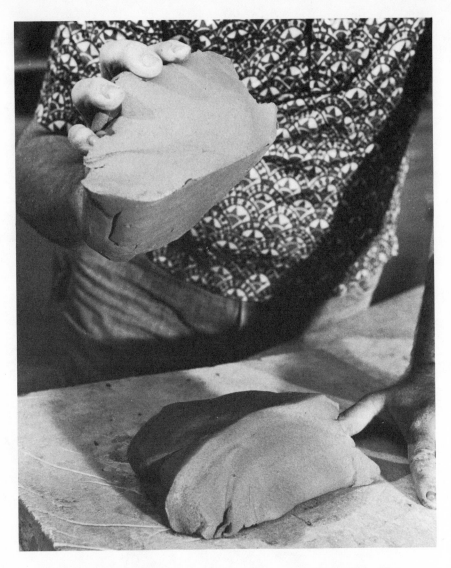

Wedging 2. Pick up one piece of the clay. Turn this piece upside-down and slam it down on the wedging board. Pick up the other piece of clay and slam it on top of the first piece with easy-to-medium force. This will join together the two smooth surfaces that were previously lying flat on your board as part of the original mass of clay. Notice that the surfaces that you first cut with the wire should be facing away from you.

Repeat this process: cut the new mass of clay in half and slam one on top of the other. Continue until the clay is of an even consistency and you cannot see any air spaces in the clay. Check this by periodically inspecting the inner surface of the clay after you have cut it in half with wire.

The wedging procedure should take anywhere from two to five minutes, depending on the efficiency you develop.

Kneading

Kneading 1. With your fingers, lift up a mass of clay starting at the edge of the large piece. Do not break this mass off, but push it up and forward so that it is sitting on top of the rest of the clay piece.

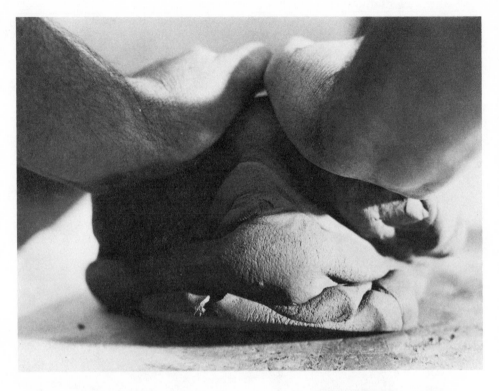

Kneading 2. Press this mass of clay down into the center of the larger piece with the heels of your hands. Continue this process for several minutes; then check the consistency by cutting the clay in half with a wire. Knead clay vigorously in this manner until it is in a suitable condition.

I encourage you to take the opportunity sometime to watch a professional potter do spiral kneading, which is even more efficient than the kneading technique demonstrated here, but is difficult to photograph in sequence with still photography.

Adding Filler

Sometimes it will be necessary to add additional filler (sand or grog) to your clay. You can tell your clay lacks filler if your pots crack and warp during drying and firing. As I mentioned previously, clay for handbuilding should have about 10-20 percent volume of sand or grog.

To add additional filler, spread a thin layer of sand on the plaster wedging surface and wedge the clay over the sand so that it becomes mixed into the clay (similar to adding flour to your bread board when kneading dough). I usually use either 30-mesh or 60-mesh sand, which should be available at your local building supplier.

Because this addition will stiffen your clay, you may need to soften the clay with water before adding filler. Moisten by dunking a mass of clay in water, or holding it under the tap. Then wedge and/or knead it. Repeat if the clay becomes too dry as you add the filler. Clay that is too dry will crack and break while wedging and kneading it.

Be careful not to add too much filler—clay with excess filler will easily crack while you are shaping it.

Paddle and Scoop Planter
—with Cacti and Succulents

Roger: This type of pot is called Paddle and Scoop because you make it by using a wooden stick, or paddle, to shape the clay into its basic form, and then scoop out the inside bowl. The examples shown here vary in height from 2″ to 3″ and in diameter from 2½″ to 3″, and so they are appropriate for many different kinds of small plants. I prefer the small cacti and succulents. The heavy, fleshy leaf of the succulent and the rough-needled texture of the cactus are both harmonious with these natural, stony planters.

Notice that these pots are glazed on the inside so that some of the dark, glassy coating drips out onto the rim of the pot. The rest of the pot is left natural and unglazed.

Raymond: Roger has constructed here a set of small planters, excellent in size for slow growers like cacti whose roots will not quickly outgrow the pot. The planter also serves well for starting off young, easily propagated growers as are some of the succulents.

The style of this planter is similar to the natural desert environment of cacti and succulents. The shape of the pot reminds me of stones you might find in the bed of an ancient desert stream.

On p. 176 I discuss how to plant cacti and succulents.

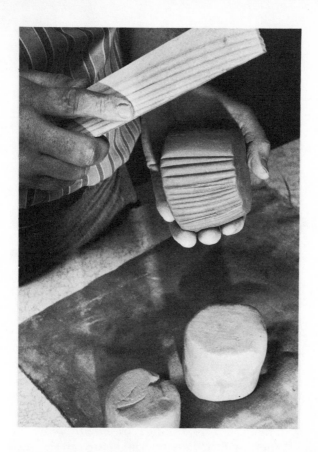

Paddle and Scoop Planter

Probably the easiest technique in this book is the paddle and scoop. The paddle method employs the flat surface of a wooden paddle to press a hunk of clay into the shape of a pot, with a firm tapping motion. The edge of the paddle is used to texture the sides of the pot. The clay inside the pot is then scooped out.

This technique is very direct, and makes a good beginning project.

A-1. Form a small piece of clay into a cylinder shape, from 2″ to 3″ high and 2½″ to 3″ in diameter. The flat side of a wooden stick will help you to paddle the sides into shape. Here I am using the same stick to texture the sides of the pot, by pressing vertical lines in the clay with the edge of the stick.

A-2. Scoop out the inside of the bowl with a wire loop tool, and leave the walls about ½″ thick. There is no need to cut a drainhole if the planter is used for cacti and other plants that need little water.

Allow the pot to become bone dry, that is, completely dry, before firing it in the kiln. This waiting period should always be observed before firing. Then glaze the pot on the inside with a dark, glossy glaze and allow some of it to drip over the outside rim of the pot, as in this example. Then fire the pot again.

Pinch Planter
—with Herbs

Raymond: This pot was a response to many students and friends wanting herb planters for centerpiece and kitchen use. Herbs are sold in nearly any plant store, or start your own from seed.

Pictured here you see parsley, upland cress and thyme. You can plant any combination of herbs, such as basil, chives, oregano, savory and mints. Just pinch off a bit when you need it for cooking or making tea. The difference in flavor between fresh and dried store-bought herbs will amaze you!

See p. 176 for an illustration of the potting technique I used for this herb planter.

Roger: This multiple planter consists of three rounded pots connected to each other. The pots are glazed on the inside, and textured on the outside. Because of drainage during watering, you will need to provide a catchplate or to put the herbs in the sink when you water them.

The triple-pot design will allow you to grow a miniature herb garden in your kitchen so that your favorites are readily available. The planter will look good on your kitchen or dining room table, or on a window sill.

Pinch Planter

This pot was made using the pinch method — pinching out the inside of each bowl-shape with your thumb and forefinger. You can make a single pot or a multiple pot as illustrated in the following sequence.

B-1. Form a mass of clay about the size you want your planter to be. Open three small bowl shapes, using your thumb to press against the inside of the bowls and stretch the clay out.

B-2. With pressure between your thumb and index finger, pinch the clay and move the clay upward from the bottom of the inside of the bowl to the rim. Try to develop a pot with wall of even thickneess. Let the pot grow equally and naturally. You may wish to carve out some of the thickness in the base of the bowl when the clay becomes leather-hard (after the clay has dried to a firm, yet still moist state; leather-hard clay would crack if bent). Repeat this process for all three bowl-shapes.

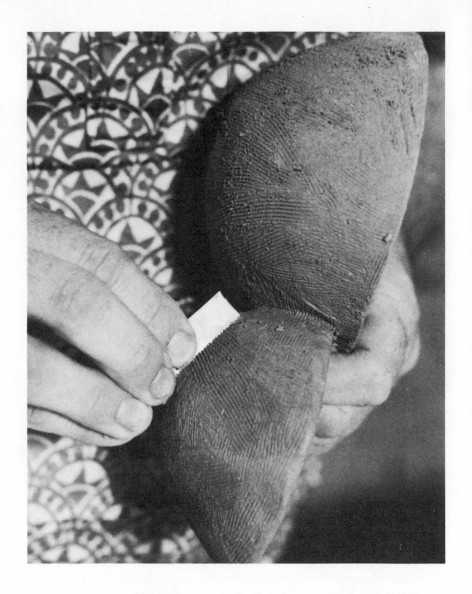

B-3. A piece of old, broken hacksaw blade may be used to level off the outside surface and leave an interesting scratched texture. A tin can lid will work well to scrape the inside of each pot.

If you want the rims of your pots to express a graceful movement, develop the rims carefully in a continuous flowing line without irregularities.

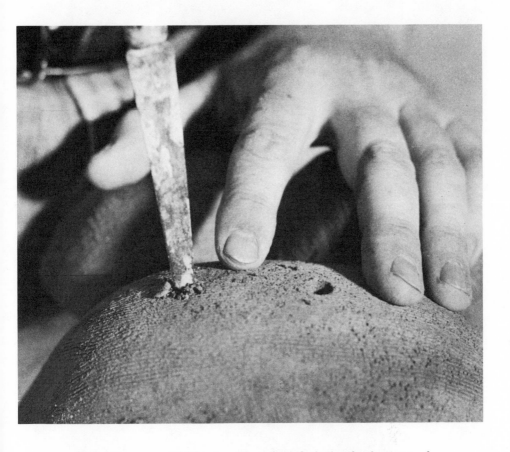

B-4. If you would like to put a drainhole in the bottom of the planter, drill a hole with a knife blade in the center of the base, twisting as you go through.

Let the pot dry. After firing it, you may wish to glaze the inside. Then fire it again.

Petal Planter
—with False Aralia

Roger: There is an elegance that this plant and planter share. Neither seems complete without the other. The scalloped, arching leaves of the False Aralia repeat the overlapping petal design of the pot. The plant is spacious and breezy-looking and the complementary airiness of the pot was achieved by opening spaces in the last two rows of petals.

This plant has a beautiful, striking profile. I applied a dark glaze so that the combined silhouettes of the pot and plant work together.

Raymond: The False Aralia (Dizygotheca elegantissima) has reddish-brown leaves, and will grow to about 18″ in height. Although Roger and I agreed from the very first when we tried the False Aralia in this pot, I still searched for other possibilities, and attempted a change at least three of four times. The real proof of the decision came the day of this photograph. The False Aralia seems to be growing effortlessly out of the pot. It's quite a graceful combination.

Petal Planter

For this planter you put to use the pinching method learned in the previous project, combined with a technique of adding clay petals.

C-1. Pinch a simple bowl, about 6″ high and 6″ in diameter (see **B-1 — B-4**).

C-2. Roll balls of clay and smash them flat, into circular petal shapes from about 1″ to 2″ in diameter. Make the petals as you need them.

C-3. With a fork or toothed blade, scratch one edge of the petals you will use for your first row. Wet them at the bottom edge where they will come in contact with the edge of the bowl. Press together the bottom edge of each petal with the inside top edge of the bowl. Repeat, placing petals side by side until you have completed the first row of petals.

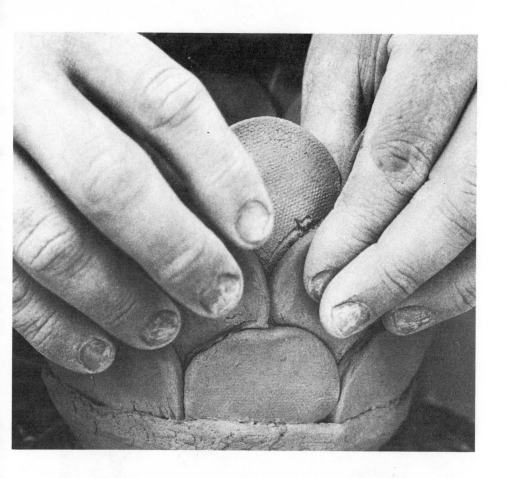

C-4. Add new petals scratching and wetting them first as above, and pressing them on the inside of the previous row. Let your pot grow row by row. This pot was made with five rows of petals.

For variety you may cut out spaces in the top two rows of petals to create an airy effect, using a needle tool.

Possible variations: You can use different petal shapes to develop different rhythmic patterns. Try slab shapes cut to various sizes (see **H-1 — H-3,** p. 95). You can stamp petals with a design (see p. 93).

Now you can let your pot dry, fire it, and then glaze it and fire again. You will notice that I glazed only the petal portion of the planter, and left the bowl at the bottom in its natural state.

Coil Planter
—with Asparagus Fern

Raymond: This is one of the containers, Roger, that you speak of as "having a need" or being open to receiving a plant. It is planted with an Asparagus sprengeri, one of the most common of the Asparagus ferns. Its shade of green goes so well with the earthen color of the vessel; and the small, needle-like leaves make an interesting match with the busy scale-pattern on the surface of the pot. In the picture you can see how the beauty of this plant's free, asymmetric form is accented by the shapely container.

Consult p. 177 for a description of how I potted this Asparagus fern and p. 192 for pruning hints.

Roger: The planter shown here is made by the coil building process, one of the oldest pottery techniques in the world. The pot surface is the result of using your fingers to make a pattern of small impressions in the clay. There is a beautiful random quality created when texturing in this manner. The freely patterned texture of the pot and the casual growth of the plant give this combination a true unity.

Coil Technique

Coil-made pottery has been the most universal technique among potters of the world throughout history. Coil technique is very versatile, and after mastering it, one can build very large and complex pieces of pottery quickly. Essentially, it consists of piling rope-like pieces of clay one on top of the other, and joining them together with your fingers.

Pottery of the past may give you ideas for your own work. If you wish to examine coil pottery done by other cultures, you need only go to any museum or look in a book on the history of ceramics. The aboriginal potters of North and South America built their pottery primarily with coils. The Incas of Peru and Ecuador used this method to make very complicated pots with anthropomorphic designs. You can also discover the beautifully controlled, symmetrical pots done in the Southwestern United States by the Pueblo Indians. The smoothness you will notice in these pots comes from scraping and burnishing the surface.

I enjoy working with coils because of the beautiful textures you can add as part of the coiling process itself (see F-1 — F-6, p. 78).

If you are doing a large coil pot, it may be necessary to allow the bottom to dry partially and stiffen a bit before continuing with the rest of the walls, since too much weight may cause the pot to collapse. You will know when the walls need stiffening: the pot will begin to sag.

As you work, keep the top edge of the uppermost coil moist by covering it with a plastic sheet, such as a dry cleaning bag or painter's dropcloth. If you let the coils dry out too much, as you begin to add more coils they will not stick well to the previous ones.

The shape of your pot will change as you increase or decrease its width with each new coil added. Avoid sudden changes in shape, though; you may create weakness and cause the pot to collapse.

You may work on your pot over a long period of time, but

wrap it in plastic each time you stop to keep the clay from drying out.

Use a banding wheel to help speed the building process. If you do not have one, work on top of a small board that you can shift around easily.

Before beginning the actual construction of the coil planter pictured here, make your first coil according to the following sequence. I prefer to make coils as I work, because making them all at once subjects them to unnecessary drying.

Making Coils

D-1. Squeeze out clay into a rough coil (a long, narrow cylinder), about 6″ long and 1″ to 1½″ wide.

D-2. Place both hands in the center of the coil, and roll the clay . . .

D-3 . . . back and forth with pressure. As you roll, draw out your hands from the center so that each hand moves to one end of the coil. If your coil becomes square or flat, slowly and carefully roll out the irregular spots so that the entire coil is equally rounded. The finished coil should be between ¼″ and ⅝″ in diameter, and about 12″ to 18″ long. Thicker coils provide easier control for beginners. Larger pots will require coils of larger diameter.

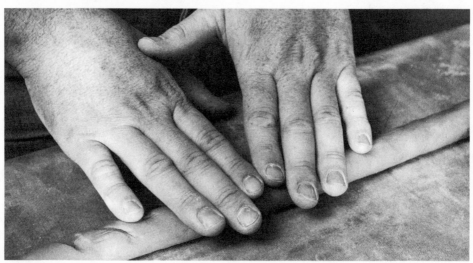

Coil Planter

E-1. Cut out a circular slab of clay, ⅜" thick and about 4" in diameter (**H-1 — H-3** p. 95, for instructions on how to cut a slab).

Place your first coil on top of this slab so that it circles the perimeter. Cut or twist the coil ends so they will be squared off, and then butt them neatly together. Smooth the joint with your finger.

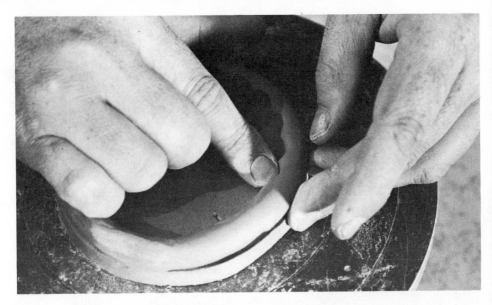

E-2. With your fingertip, press the inside edge of the coil downward so the clay spreads onto the base. Do this all around the inside circumference. Support the outside of the coil with your other hand as you do this, so that you will not change the coil's original position.

E-3. Repeat the process on the outside of the coil, pressing the edge downward to the base. Remember to support the inside now as you work on the outside.

E-4. Continue to place one coil on the top of the previous one in this manner. Here I have used 25 coils to make a pot about 11″ high. The fingertip pressure will join the coils together and at the same time create an interesting pattern on the outside surface of the pot.

If you wish to develop a wider diameter in the pot, set the next coil on the outside edge of the previous coil. To make the diameter smaller, set the next coil on the inside edge of the previous one.

E-5. Trim the base to finish the form and make it visually more buoyant.

E-6. In this instance, a thick coil was placed on top to make the rim, and the texture of the sides of the pot was modified by paddling the surface lightly.

Let the pot dry thoroughly before firing it.

Hanging Coil Planter
— with Piggyback

Raymond: I like this planter for its dynamic shape and massiveness. It offers a very dramatic presentation to its plant subject, the Piggyback. The Piggyback plant is a member of the Saxifrage family, and derives its name from the fact that the younger plants grow out of the mature leaves of the parent plant. This plant thrives in a semi-shaded area in a well drained pot with rich soil.

For advice on how to keep your Wandering Jew well pruned so that it keeps its stylish shape, see p. 196.

Roger: This hanging planter is unusual in that it does not have a flat base. The bottom was made with three openings to create an interesting effect, since the pot will be hanging above eye level. The openings in the base are also useful for water drainage and aeration. You can use your imagination to make hanging planters with decorative bottoms.

Another unusual aspect of this pot is that it was made upside-down, starting with the rim first. You will observe more clearly in the photographs to follow that the rim does not have a conventional circular shape, but is indented rather like a clover-leaf.

The coil technique used in making this planter lends itself to a variety of textured designs. First I will present a sequence on texture variations you can consider for your coil planters, and then in the following sequence I will describe the making of this hanging planter.

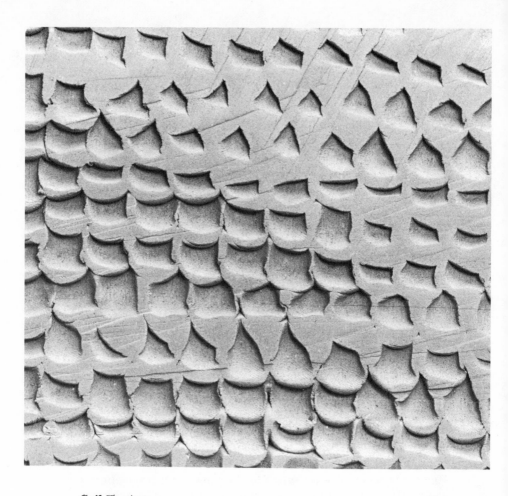

Coil Textures

Undoubtedly you have become aware of the random scale pattern created with the tip of your finger when you push the clay coils together to build a pot. There is a variety of patterns you can consciously create to decorate your planter. Think of the pattern in relation to the kind of plant you will be using. The designs can enrich the surface of the pot to complement or harmonize with your plant.

Here are several different scale patterns you can use.

F-1. This photo illustrates a random scale pattern that was heavily paddled with a flat stick.

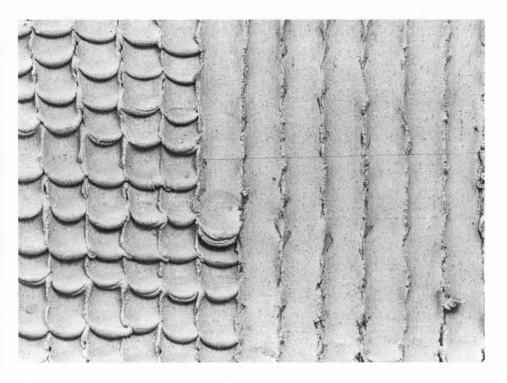

F-2. The left side of the photo shows a vertical series of scales. On the right side, the scales were scraped together by running a fingertip vertically down the clay to form grooves, leaving a strong fluted effect.

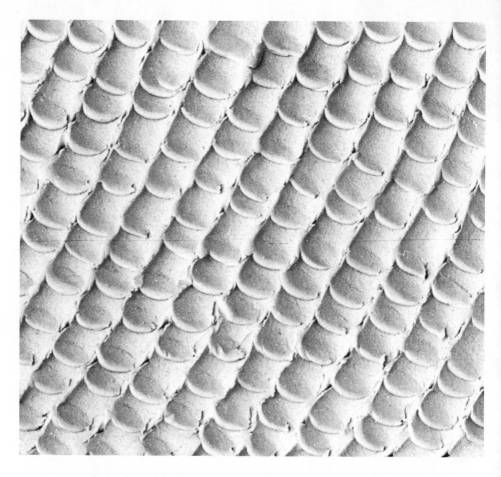

F-3. The horizontal coils were pulled together with a diagonal finger stroke, thus creating diagonal scales. This will give a pot a dynamic spiraling surface.

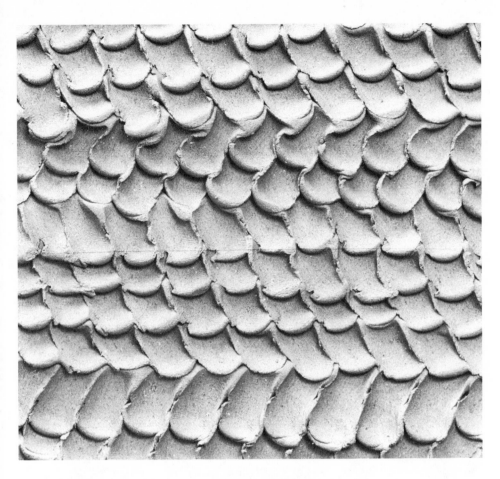

F-4. Herringbone (zig-zag) scale pattern.

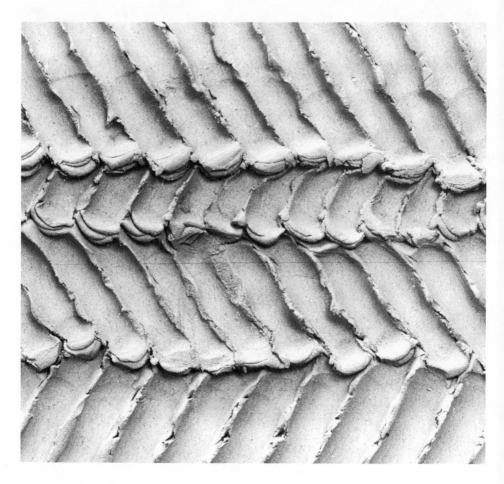

F-5. A herringbone pattern with scales run together by scraping with a fingertip, as in **F-2** above.

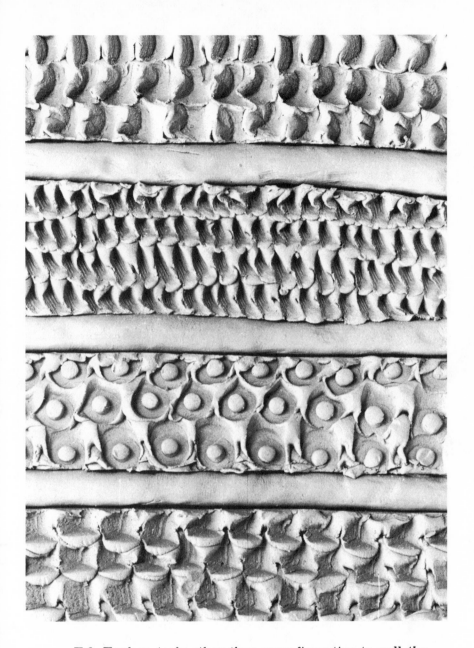

F-6. Explore tools other than your fingertips to pull the coils together, such as a knife blade or handle, a wooden stick, or any object that will make a mark in clay. Every tool will make a different texture.

Hanging Coil Planter

To make a hanging coil planter as pictured, on p. **76**, follow this sequence.

G-1. Starting with the rim, place your first coil (about ½″ in diameter) onto a board. Shape this rim coil into a cloverleaf design, as illustrated.

G-2. Follow the same coil instructions given in **E-2 — E-4**, p. 72, forming the coils to assume the same clover-shape as the rim. Let the pot grow row by row.

G-3. Close off your pot by gradually decreasing its diameter. Develop three openings for water drainage and aeration. You can see how the edges of the openings rise up from the body of the pot like three mouths. The photo shows the clay around the mouths being textured with a piece of hacksaw blade. Notice that the coiled texture of the pot has been paddled with a stick, smoothing the surface partially.

G-4. After the bottom is done and the pot is allowed to become firm (leather-hard) the pot is turned upright and the top rim is finished. I an holding the pot in my lap and paddling the rim with a stick. Then three small holes are carved into the sides of the pot with a knife so that the ropes that will hang the planter can pass through.

Allow your pot to dry; then it can be fired.

Variation Coil Planter with Spider Plant

Roger: Flamboyant would be the right adjective to describe this planter. It was made similarly to the hanging coil planter. However, the coils are textured into a diagonal scale design. After allowing the clay to become leather-hard, I cleaned out the individual scales by running them together to form grooves, as shown in **F-2 — F-3** (p. 78), thereby creating spirals.

The bottom of the planter is flat, so that the pot can sit upright or be hung. The surface of the pot is stained with dark Barnard Clay, which creates a striking contrast between the green and white plant and the container (see the description of how to apply Barnard Clay on p. 169).

Raymond: We were thrilled to see the combination of this planter and a large variegated Chlorophytum. They share an elegance and a "show-off" style that is ageless, transcending all periods and styles of architecture and furnishings. The diagonal lines moving around the pot are similar to the strongly curved, long leaves of this large spider plant.

Slab Box Planter
—with Cobra-Leaf Plectranthus

Raymond: Ordinarily you'd have to plant this Cobra-Leaf Plectranthus in a hanging pot to give its leaves room to stretch down. But this tall pot makes it possible to set the plant on a table because it provides enough room for the long hanging stems so they don't become bent and mashed.

The slab box planter is a good example of how to face the challenge of a pot that has no drainhole. I have invented a device you can use, called the Bridwell Sleeve. It will hold the plant's roots together so they won't wash away, and will also make insertion into a tall container such as this one easier (the pot also has a rather small opening at the top). I'm not aware of any other horticulturalist who uses this method to pot houseplants. I've written a section for this book, starting on p. 178, to show you how to make the Bridwell Sleeve and plant this subject.

Roger: If you look carefully at the design on the bottom half of this planter, you will see that it is suggestive of young growing plants. The design was made using a stamp that I carved myself; the stamp is used to press designs into clay.

Stamping is particularly appropriate for planters made by the slab box method of construction, as this planter was. In this section I include sequences on the technique of making slabs, as well as the technique of making your own stamps.

I enjoy the contrast of this stamped, textured design with the smooth, glazed white upper portion of the planter. The white of the glazed surface relates beautifully to the off-white in the leaf pattern of the plant.

I was delighted to find that I could build tall planters like this one (approximately 8″ tall and 6″ wide) without drainholes and horrid little platters to catch the drainage. The sleeve device that Raymond designed has opened up many other possibilities for planter shapes that I previously thought were impossible to use.

Slab Technique

Slabs are like solid walls of clay that are fitted together. They are easy to cut and join, and provide the potter with forms unattainable by any other construction technique. Pottery made with slabs often has a crisp angularity of shape akin to architectural forms, and in fact you may use architectural forms as an inspiration for slab planter shapes.

Most handbuilt pottery relies heavily upon the flexible and plastic nature of the clay, since the potter makes his shapes from an amorphous mass of material. Slab pots are very different. They are usually fabricated with somewhat stiff, leather-hard sheets of clay that have been pre-cut to various shapes.

Two very important considerations in slab construction are:

(1). The amount of filler (sand or grog) in the clay. Usually it is necessary that clay contain somewhere between 10-20 percent filler to aid in even drying throughout the wall of the clay form. This lessens warping and cracking problems. If you need to add more filler to stiffen up the slabs, follow the instructions in the section on Wedging (p. 45).

(2). The amount of moisture in the clay slab. Often you will need to dry your clay to a leather-hard stage before the slabs can be assembled (leather-hard means stiff yet still somewhat moist). However, you must not allow the clay to dry too much; assembly then becomes impossible because the joints between the slabs will not adhere. The best advice here is to assemble the pot as soon as the clay slabs can be handled without bending or creating distortion.

Stamping Textures in Slab Walls

The smooth wall surface of the slab lends itself to a wide variety of designs. In this photo you can see a number of possibilities made by pressing different kinds of stamps into the soft clay.

You can make stamps out of almost anything. Here you

see a plaster wheel (a cylinder) into which designs have been carved. To make one, first mix up a batch of casting plaster (see the instructions on p. 124, **J-1 — J-4**). Pour the plaster into a cardboard tube and allow the plaster to set; then remove the cardboard and carve your design with a knife. The plaster wheel is rolled across the surface of the clay slab, impressing patterns as it goes. You can also carve the round end of the plaster cylinder, and stamp a pattern into the clay, as pictured.

Another example shown here is a clay stamp (it looks like a mushroom with a design on top). Form the general shape out of clay, and then carve a design in it. After you fire the stamp once in the kiln, it is ready to use.

Other stamps include a bamboo brush handle and a broken plaster chip. In fact you can experiment with almost any utensil or object that will make an interesting pattern when pressed into clay.

Besides using stamps to create textures, try making patterns by using tools such as a serrated blade pulled across the clay, or a loop tool to cut wavy lines. Invent your own personal vocabulary of textures by exploring tools and objects you have on hand.

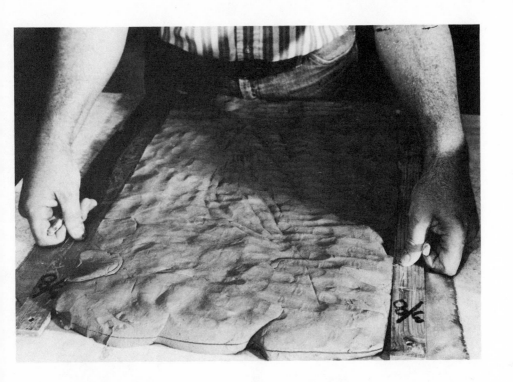

Slab Box Planter

H-1. On a piece of canvas or burlap, spread out a sheet of clay at least 8″ x 10″ and ½″ thick or more. Take two wooden sticks, ⅜″ thick each, and place one on each side of the clay sheet, running lengthwise. Hold a cutting wire stretched between your hands so that the wire is at the height of the two guide sticks. Pull the cutting wire from the far end of the clay through the middle, toward you, so that you are slicing the clay slab crosswise into two pieces. The slab on the bottom will be ⅜″ thick.

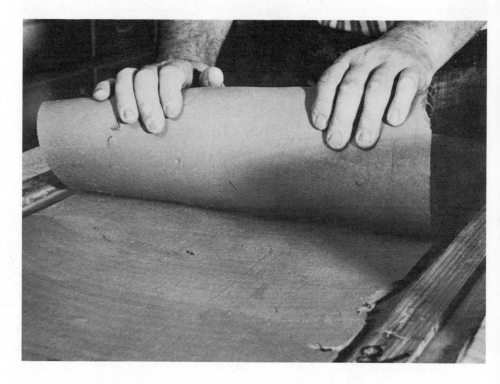

H-2. Remove the top layer of clay by rolling it back. Use the bottom ⅜″ thick slab for the construction of the slab planter. You will be making as many of these ⅜″ slabs as you will need for all sides of the planter box—in this case, 6 (4 for the walls and one each for the base and top). Each wall in this example will be approximately 6″ x 8″ and the base and top slabs are about 7″ x 7″.

H-3. Before cutting the slab to the shape you need, you may use plaster texture wheels, stamps, or other objects to make impressions in the clay (as described in the preceding sequence). Here I am rolling the plaster wheel across what will become the bottom edge of one wall of the planter. However, you can stamp your design anywhere on the slab's surface.

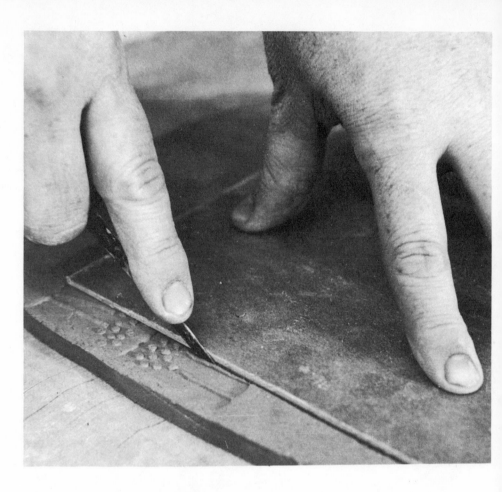

H-4. To cut out the size slab you will need for each wall, you can use a piece of cardboard cut to the size of each wall.

Cut around the perimeter of the cardboard with a knife. Then peel the clay slab off the canvas. Do this four times for the four walls. Do the same for the top and bottom slabs.

H-5. The edges of the walls have to be cut on a 45″ angle. This is necessary so that the edges of all the walls will fit closely together, and to be sure that the stamped design meets evenly when all four walls are joined. To cut the edges, use a knife and a straight edge (a ruler) as a guide.

After cutting, allow the clay to become leather-hard (stiff, yet not dry). Clay slabs that are too dry will not join well; clay slabs that are too wet will be limp and difficult to handle.

H-6. Scratch the surface of the angled edges of each slab with a fork or other tool. This helps the joints between the slabs to adhere more strongly when you put the slabs together.

H-7. Brush the surfaces of the edges of the four walls with a coat of clay slip. Clay slip is a loose mixture of clay with liberal amount of water. The slip will help the joints of the walls stick together.

H-8. Place the edges of two of the walls together with a firm yet gentle pressure. To do this, let one wall rest flat on a surface, and hold the other wall vertically. Place the two edges together as shown. Slide the vertical wall back and forth until the joint between the two walls is firm and clay slip oozes out along the joint.

H-9. Check all along the outside corners where the two walls are joined, and push the clay together to seal any openings. Be careful not to mar the designed areas while working on the joints.

H-10. After wiping the inside joint with a sponge, roll a coil of clay. Push the coil in all along the inside joint to reinforce it. Then smooth out the coil with your finger, as shown. Repeat steps **H-8 — H-10** until all four walls are joined together.

H-11. Assemble all four walls on top of the leather-hard slab you have cut for the base. Be sure to stick the new joints together as described above.

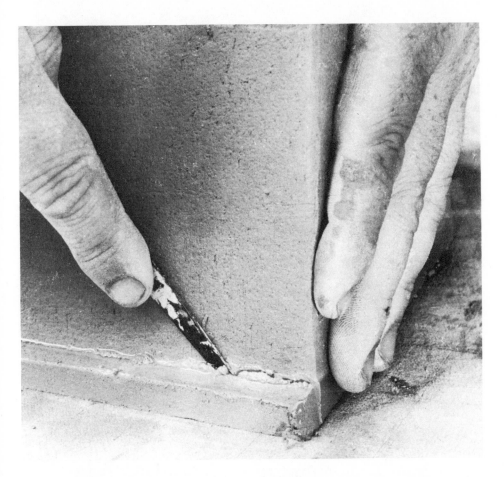

H-12. After you have secured the bottom slab to the walls, trim off the excess clay that extends out past the walls with a knife.

Turn the box upside down and repeat this process for the slab that goes on top of the box, sticking the joints together and trimming off the excess.

H-13. Cut out a hole in the top of the box, about 5″ in diameter. Here I am keeping the circle from falling in by holding it with a needle tool as I cut out the top with a knife.

H-14. An old hacksaw blade may be used to clean up irregular areas around the circular opening on top of the planter. The blade marks may be left as an interesting texture, or they may be smoothed over.

Check all the slab joints to see that they are secure, and touch up the outside walls of the planter if needed.

After letting this planter dry and firing it, you can glaze the top half of the pot (starting above the stamped design) as I did, using a smooth white glaze. Then fire it again.

Explore other combinations of proportion, texture and glaze application.

Variation:

Curved Slab Box Planter with Crassula Tetragona

Roger: The planter in this photograph is constructed with a slab box technique, but the box is shorter and broader than the preceding planter. The sides have been heavily textured, using a loop tool to cut wavy lines. The slightly curved effect was achieved by paddling the corners with a stick to soften the form.

Raymond: You can see that these two go together—the delicate texture and flatness of the pot, and leaf shape and flat growth characteristics of the Crassula Tetragona. You could not ask for a better match.

This is another of the no-drainhole pots. Simply water this plant very lightly and depend on the plant to remove the water from the soil in its normal growth.

Modular Planter
—with Palm

Roger: This planter is constructed of multiple units, or modules. They are curved slabs of clay that have been joined together. The style expresses a formal grace similar to the lines of a Greek column. To enhance this architectural resemblance, the exterior of the pot was not glazed, but left plain. Only the interior was given a glossy coating.

The palm chosen for this pot goes well with the modular design of the planter. The palm also consists of modular units, and it too has a certain formality about it.

The most interesting aspect of the combination is the way the light and shadow play across the surface of the planter and the palm.

Raymond: As you will recall, Roger, I had brought several plants into the studio one day, among them this Neanthe Bella palm. As you left your clay work and walked by the table, you placed the palm in the container and the selection was made unanimously.

Modular Planter

The box is a strong architectural shape and is an obvious way to use slabs. But slab construction need not be limited to a box shape.

The following planter is also architectural in concept, but uses slabs curved into a half-cylinder shape. The duplicate units were then joined together to form a uniquely shaped container.

Explore similar modules, arranging them in different ways. Use units of various shapes, push your imagination, and be open to new possibilities for future pots.

I-1. Cut 10 slabs, approximately 5" x 5" (use the technique shown in **H-1, H-2,** and **H-4,** p. 95). Bend the slabs around a cylinder before they dry. A 12oz. orange juice can being used in this case. If your clay cracks, it is either too dry and not plastic enough, or you are bending it too far. Try softening the clay by sprinkling it with water.

I-2. Experiment with different arrangements of these slab forms. After final placement has been decided, scratch two marks on the top of each slab with a pencil (one mark on each end), so that you will be able to match the marks together as you reassemble the slabs. This will ensure that you have them in their correct position.

I-3. With a fork, scratch vertical lines along the sides where the slabs will join together. Then liberally coat the scratched surfaces with clay slip (clay mixed with a lot of water to form a paste).

I-4. Return the slabs to their original arrangement and press the joints together firmly, using the pencil marks as a guide. After assembly, use a pencil or sharp stick to clean out the excess clay slip from the crevices.

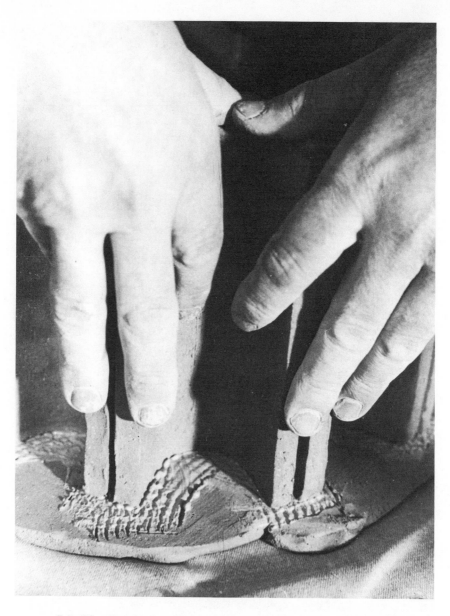

I-5. The finished walls must now be placed onto a circular slab larger than the outside diameter of your construction. This will form the base of the planter. First scratch the slab and apply clay slip where the walls will make contact. Then stick the walls to the base firmly.

I-6. To assist you in turning your planter upside-down so you can work on the bottom, sandwich the planter in between two boards and then flip.

I-7. Trim off the excess clay on the bottom slab with a needle tool or a fettling knife. Reinforce all the joints of the slabs with a coil of clay (as in **H-10,** p. 104). Then smooth out undesired irregularities along the edges with a hacksaw blade (see **H-13,** p. 106). You can use a pencil to clean the hard-to-get-at crevices.

You are now finished with the form. Allow it to dry; then fire it. I chose not to glaze the exterior because I didn't want the texture of a glaze to compete with the strong architectural quality of the planter.

Spherical Mold Planter
—with Swedish Ivy and Wandering Jew

Raymond: Putting two kinds of plants in one pot (companion planting) seems to be quite popular. I like the sassiness of the glossy, bright green Swedish Ivy (or Creeping Charlie) against the rich green and plum tones of the Wandering Jew.

These plants go well with the sphere-shape of the pot. If you used a too rounded plant, the two together would have such a ball shape that if they ever got away, they would roll half a block! The Swedish Ivy and Wandering Jew are able to drape their long stems down the sides of the sphere.

Companion planting can be done with many different varieties. Just be careful not to mix two plants that have very different needs for light and water — or you'll have a schizophrenic pair.

See my comments on pruning this plant combination, on p. 196.

Roger: Illustrated here is a general principle you can follow in fitting pot to plant: by repeating a motif, you strengthen the visual unity between the two. Notice the S-curve designs on the planter. They are reflected in the S-curves of the stems of both plants, as they arch out from the planter.

This spherical planter is an example of a form you can make by using a mold—in this case, a child's ball—which gives the clay its globe-shape. I will explain the use of molds in the following sequence, and show you how to make your own molds out of plaster.

Molds

A mold is a hollow form into which you can put soft clay. The clay will harden to the particular shape of the mold.

Molds have been used in pottery making for thousands of years. The earliest potters spread clay into baskets. These baskets were often placed in a campfire, and after the baskets were completely burned away, only a shell of clay in the shape of the basket remained. Some historians contend this was the invention of pottery. Who is to know! In any case, this does represent a very early mold technique of pottery.

Today we don't use molds made out of baskets, but out of plaster. A plaster mold is made from another shape, such as a ball or bowl, around which the liquid plaster sets and hardens. After removing this object from the plaster, clay can be placed inside the plaster mold and left to dry. When the clay becomes leather-hard and easy to handle without deforming, the clay shape is lifted out of the plaster mold and mold can be used again.

Instead of making a plaster mold, you can use a bowl as a mold, placing cheesecloth on the inside surface before

putting clay into the form. The cheesecloth will keep the clay from sticking to the inside of the bowl.

To make a mold, you can use almost any shape that you can find in your kitchen, children's toy box or garage. This photo shows a few examples — bowls of various sizes, a baking pan, and a cylindrical oatmeal box.

Molds can open up the possibility of many new shapes which could not be built any other way. Mold forms can also be combined with other techniques, such as coils, as in the coil sphere planter we will describe.

The following sequence will demonstrate the making of a plaster hemisphere mold. You will be able to build many different pots from its simple shape.

Making a Plaster Hemisphere Mold

Mixing plaster is not a technically difficult process. If you follow carefully the following steps, you can mix a good batch every time.

Have all your materials at hand so you will be able to proceed without difficulty. You may purchase casting plaster (it is in powder form) from your ceramic dealer or local building supplier. Be sure to have plenty of water available. Don't put plaster down the sink; wash up in a separate bucket.

You will need a plastic bucket big enough to hold a child's ball, which is the shape you will use for your mold. The bucket I am using here is approximately 12" in diameter and 9" deep. The ball is about 10" in diameter. Be sure that the bucket is larger at the rim than at the base, so that you will be able to remove your plaster mold easily after is sets.

You will also need some petroleum jelly (vaseline). Before mixing the plaster, smear a thin film of petroleum jelly on the inside surface of the bucket, and then wipe out the excess with a rag or paper towel.

Let's now begin the plaster mixing.

J-1. Fill the bucket about ⅓ full with water. Take a handful of casting plaster and sift it through your fingers, letting plaster fall on the water as you move your hand over its surface. You will notice how the plaster falls to the bottom as it absorbs water.

J-2. Keep sifting plaster into the water in this manner, and soon you will see islands of dry plaster floating on the surface. Add plaster until the whole surface is covered with plaster, like one large island. When the surface is completely covered, stop putting plaster in. Allow the mixture to sit for about one minute, until the dry surface plaster is absorbed in the water.

J-3. Now stir the mixture with your hand (you can wear a rubber glove), working out the lumps. Keep your hand low in the bucket and avoid rapid stirring, which will create undesirable air bubbles in the mix.

J-4. When you feel a homogenous mix, tap or bounce the container to encourage any air bubbles in the plaster to rise. Then place your ball into the plaster mixture, so that it is covered halfway. Do not put petroleum jelly on the ball. It will come out easily since it is flexible and only immersed halfway. Petroleum jelly would adversely affect the interior of the mold.

J-5. You will need some weights to keep the ball half-immersed in the plaster. Ask someone to help you hold the ball in place as you put the weights on top. Here I am using some wooden boards weighed down with bricks.

Depending on the thickness of your mix and the setting time of your plaster, you should let the mold dry for one half hour or more before you remove the ball. After taking the ball out, turn the bucket over and tap the rim on the floor. The mold should fall out of the greased bucket. It is a good idea to scrape the sharp mold edges smooth with a knife, so the plaster won't chip off and get into your clay. Allow the mold to dry in a warm place, preferably for several days, before use.

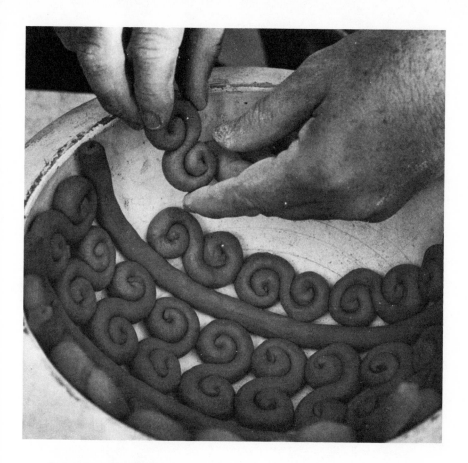

Spherical Mold Planter

Now that you have cast your hemispherical mold, you will be able to use it in a limitless variety of ways. The following sequence uses this mold with clay coils, to form intricate S-designs on the outside of the planter.

You can also use a bowl covered with cheesecloth instead of a plaster mold for this planter.

K-1 Make clay coils (shown in **D-1 — D-3, p. 69**). Arrange them in an imaginative design inside the plaster mold. I am using double S-spirals, combined with straight sections of coil. Press balls of clay into the spaces between the coils, and add clay to build up the rim to the edge of the mold.

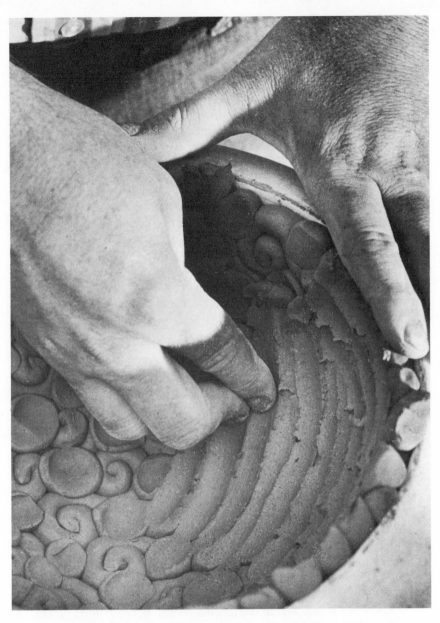

K-2. Smear the coils of clay together inside the hemisphere, using your fingers to make it one continuous piece. Be gentle, though; too much presure will destroy the coil patterns on the outside of the hemisphere too.

K-3. Trim the rim with a knife.

K-4. Allow the clay to become leather-hard, and as soon as it shrinks away from the sides of the mold, lift the clay out of the mold and keep it from drying further by wrapping it with a sheet of plastic. If placed in the sun, the clay will release itself from the mold in about half an hour. If placed out of the draft and in the shade, it may take hours before shrinking free.

K-5. The second half of the planter is made in similar fashion, except that this hemisphere has a circular hole left in the middle, about 5'' in diameter.

Scratch the rims of both hemispheres with a fork. Then brush clay slip on the rims (as in **H-6 — H-7**, p. 100). Place the halves together with firm pressure. Strengthen the joint by placing a coil along the inside seam (as in **H-10**, p. 104).

K-6. A fettling knife can be used to eliminate the seam's edges on the outside, and do the final cleaning.

Dry and then fire the planter. You can glaze the inside of the pot—an exterior glaze might deemphasize your attractive coil work.

Possible variations: Use this technique for bowls, compotes, woven planters with handles, or hanging baskets (using one hemisphere). Try small balls, large balls, narrow slabs, wide slabs, strips of clay crossed, strips woven, etc.

Variation 1:

Hanging Hemisphere Planter with Plectranthus Africanus

Roger: The planter shown here was made similar to the spherical mold planter except that only one hemisphere mold was used instead of two joined together. The planter should be hung high so that you can enjoy the coil patterns on the bottom.

Raymond: The globe-shape of this pot defies any plant tall and slender, and would not go well with a "roundy-moundy" plant either. The Plectranthus you see here suits the pot perfectly. It has a lateral, scaffold growth habit—the leaves stretch out over the sides of the pot without drooping down. Roger, I remember distinctly when you saw the plant you exclaimed over its beauty and leaf-shape, and the way its form suited the pot so well.

For some pruning hints, see p. 197.

135

Variation 2:

High-Footed Bowl Planter with Spider Plant

Roger: This planter is a variation of the technique shown in the K-sequence. The main technical difference is the addition of a slab-formed base or foot (for instructions on making this base, see **L-1 — L-2**, p. 143).

Raymond: I like this pot because here we have a half-sphere container which will hold a nice-sized plant, but the stem of the pot takes minimal space at table or floor level.

Variation 3:

Woven Bowl

   Roger: The planter pictured here is constructed with slab strips that were placed in the hemisphere mold in a woven pattern, and then pressed together. When the clay became leather-hard, the woven form was removed from the mold and a slab was placed on the rim and on the base to finish the pot. It was then fired, glazed, and fired again.

Variation 4:

Open Coil Planter with Melon Peperomia

Roger: A hemisphere mold was used to support the coils of this planter as they were drying. An open-work structure of this type requires very careful handling until it is fired. After your planter is glazed, it will have a great deal of structural strength. This planter serves a dual purpose—it can sit on a surface or be hung from the ceiling by running a cord through the lattice-work.

Raymond: Roger constructed this pot especially to help show the use of live sphagnum moss in planting. Many of the readers have probably seen this moss used only with hanging baskets. It is also, by the way, the type of moss used in the Bridwell Sleeve. Look at p. 186 for the special potting technique I've used here.

The Melon Peperomia you see has a cluster of large, silver-striped leaves whose graceful curves are repeated in the open work of the planter.

Lamp Planter
(Core Mold)
—with Asparagus Fern and Wandering Jew

Roger: This planter combines a plant pot with a lamp in its base. The long stems of the Asparagus fern dip down into the light, adding to the dramatic effect of the lamp. The fern has a wispiness that contrasts with the very stable cylindrical form of the planter. With the fern is planted a Wandering Jew, which gives visual relief from the busy leaf structure of the fern.

The planter is built with the aid of a core mold (a mold placed on the inside of the pot to support the clay during construction). The following sequence will demonstrate the use of a core mold.

Raymond: The Wandering Jew you see here is of the Zebrina type, and the fern is an Asparagus springeri. What a lovely pair they make! The tiny beams of light that stream out from the bottom of the planter are like the tiny needles that grow out from the stems of the Asparagus fern.

For special instructions on how I kept these companion plants well-groomed, see p. 198.

141

Lamp Planter

This sequence will show you how to use a core mold. This technique involves placing a mold in the core of the pot for support during construction. After you have successfully made the planter shown, consider the possibility of making a larger pot for the garden, using the same technique.

Core molds may be made out of materials other than plaster. The mold used here is a cylinder. You can use a large pipe, an oatmeal carton, a cardboard tube, or almost any firm cylindrical shape.

The lamp planter shown here is designed to throw small spots of light onto a wall or onto the undersides of the leaves of the plant above it.

L-1. Begin by making a large slab, about 12″ x 25″ (as shown in **H-1 — H-2,** p. 95). Cover the outside of the core cylinder you are using with paper towels, newspaper, or cloth. Lift the clay slab with the canvas it is resting on, and wrap the slab around the cylinder; then peel the canvas away from the clay. Use a straight edge to cut off the overlapping clay at the seam, as pictured.

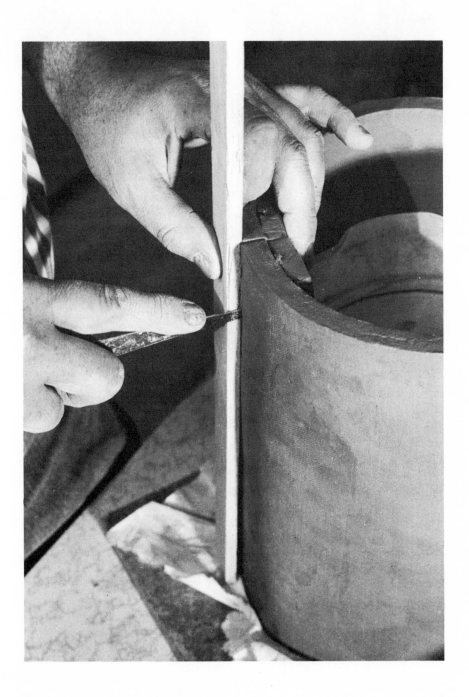

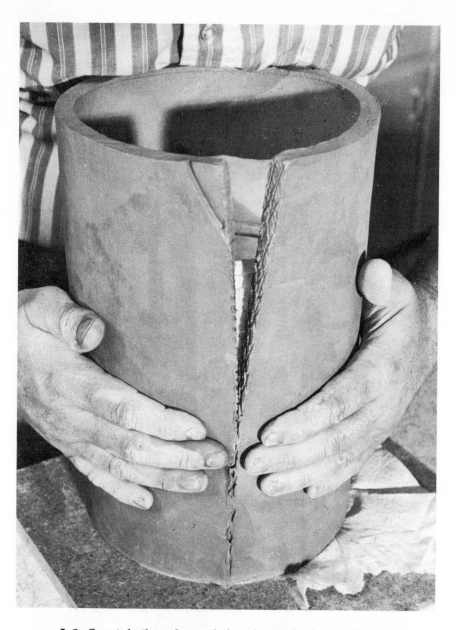

L-2. Scratch the edges of the clay cylinder at the seam, and brush on clay slip (as in **H-6 — H-7**, p. 100). Then press the adjoining edges of the seam together. Smooth the joint with the side of your knife.

L-3. Let the clay dry and firm a bit. Drying time will be affected by the amount of heat present in the room. Then push out the core cylinder (you may need assistance with this process). The paper sleeve wrapped around the core mold will allow it to slide out easily.

L-4. Cut two circular slabs, each one larger than the diameter of the ends of the cylinder. Place one slab on the bottom of the clay cylinder. Join the end of the cylinder and the base together, as in L-2 above. Reinforce the joint with a coil (as shown in **H-10,** p. 104).

Cut the cylinder into two halves, one stacking on the other. Place the second circular slab of clay on the bottom of the top half of the cylinder, in the same manner as above.

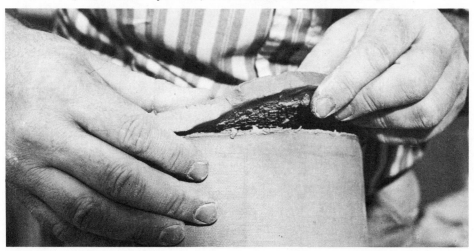

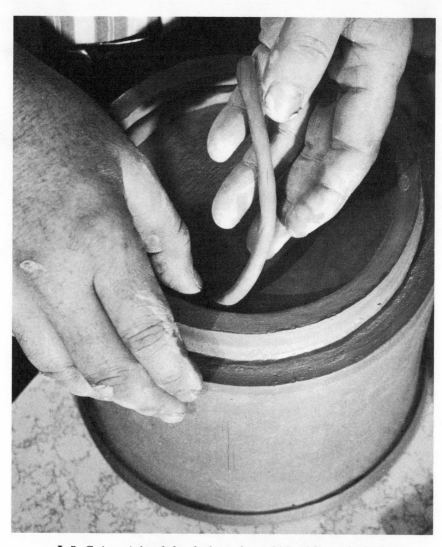

L-5. Cut a strip slab of clay about ½″ wide and 12″ long. Bend this slab into a circle, joining the seams together by scratching the ends and applying clay slip. Then attach this to the base of the top cylinder. This will form a sleeve which fits into the hollow bottom cylinder of the planter, so that the top half rests securely on the bottom half. Reinforce this sleeve with a coil. Then add a strip of clay to the top of the bottom half of the cylinder, on the outside, to create a wide rim.

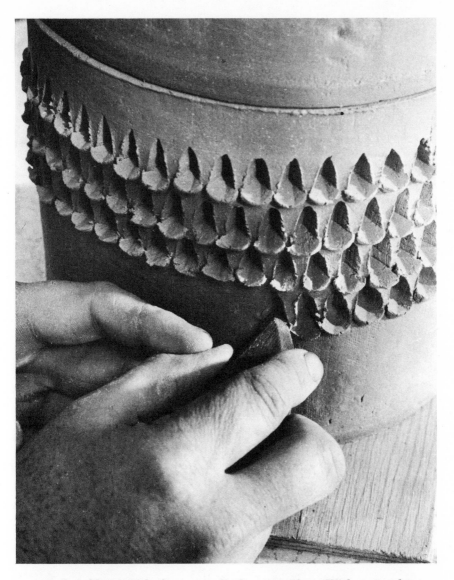

L-6. Now stack the two cylinders together. With a wooden stick, mark a pattern in the bottom cylinder for the lamp's holes. After the pattern is finished, the sharpened handle end of a needle tool can be used to pierce through each mark. These holes form a design which animates the surface of the pot and serves the function of allowing light to beam out of the base.

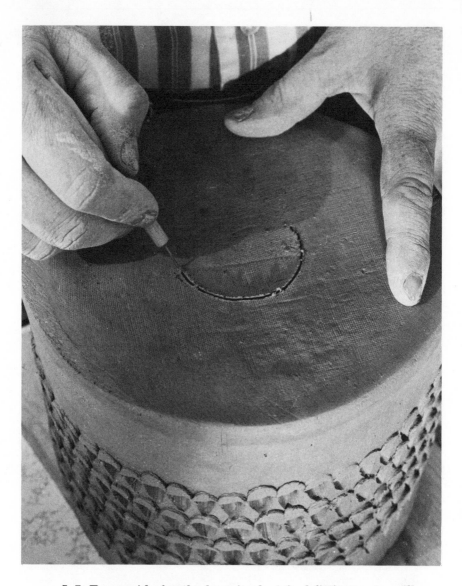

L-7. To provide for the lamp's electrical fittings, you will need to make a recessed area on the base of the bottom cylinder. Turn the bottom cylinder upside down and cut out a circle about 2″ in diameter. Cover the hole with a clay slab larger than the hold just cut. Press this slab down around its perimeter, to form a recessed circular area, as shown.

L-8. Cut out a hole about ½″ in diameter in the recessed area. This is where the rod will pass through that will hold the lamp assembly. Also make a small hole for the electrical cord on the side wall near the base of the lamp.

Dry the pot and then fire it. You can glaze it or leave it unglazed except for the inside of the planter section and a band of glaze on the upper rim, as I have done.

Local hardware or electrical shops will be able to supply parts as well as give you advice on what kind of lamp to put into the bottom half of this cylindrical planter.

Variation:

Tall Cylinder with Wandering Jew

Roger: Wandering Jew graces the top of these two cylinders. The upper portion of each cylinder is glazed. The cylinder is made like the previous one, except that there is no lamp; it is one piece.

Raymond: I've used the Bridwell Sleeve to pot this small-leafed Wandering Jew. The Bridwell Sleeve technique is described on p. 178, where I show it being used for the slab box planter.

Double Planter
(Drape Mold)
—with Crinkle-Leaf Peperomia

Raymond: I have been intrigued by this symmetrical double planter. Its smooth surface seems to demand the strong contrast of the crinkled leaves of the Peperomia. The shiny glaze on the yoke of the planter matches the glossiness of the foliage.

Roger: If you placed a tall plant in this pot there would be a very unstable feeling; and a viney plant would hang down and obscure the sculptural quality of the container. This bushy, rather low-profile Peperomia is just the right scale and proportion. The plant's leaf shape repeats the oval shape of the two halves of the planter.

The planter was made using a variation on the mold process, called the drape mold. A slab of clay was draped into a mold and allowed to take its new shape. The two pots made by this drape mold process were yoked together with a slab to form a double planter, and only the yoke was glazed.

Double Planter

This double planter uses drape mold units that have been duplicated. The units may be combined in ways different from the one shown here.

The mold was made by pressing a plastic elliptical bubble (which I found at a local craft supply store) into a mix of prepared plaster. This is similar to the way the child's ball was used in the spherical planter (see the **J** sequence, p. 124).

Find your own forms to press into plaster; they will make your pottery more individual. Avoid complex shapes because they actually limit your possibilities. Also avoid making plaster molds that will be narrower at the neck than at any other part of the shape; it will be impossible to lift the clay out of the set plaster without damaging its shape.

M-1. Cut a slab of clay of a size that will fit into your mold (as in **H-1 — H-2**). Press the slab down into the plaster mold. Then trim the excess clay from around the top of the mold with a knife. Allow the clay to become leather-hard and loose in the plaster mold; then lift the form out. Wrap the form in plastic to keep it from drying. Now make a duplicate elliptical form.

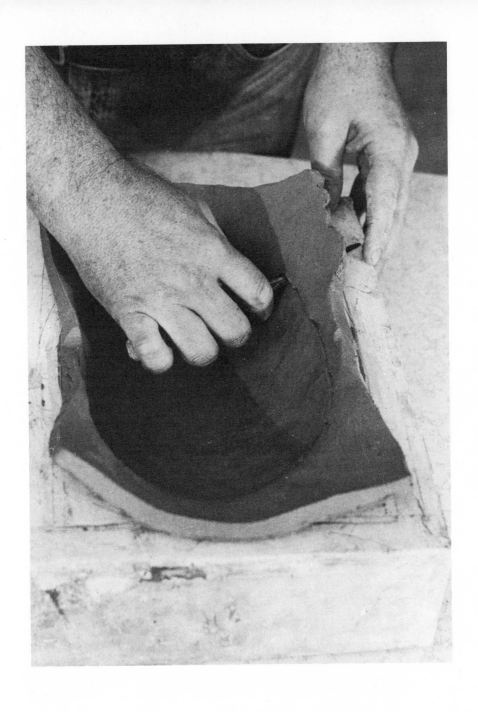

M-2. Scratch the rims of both bowls and coat them with clay slip (see **H-6 — H7**, p. 100). Then turn one bowl upside down, and place the two bowls together, rim to rim. Clean the seam with a damp spong.

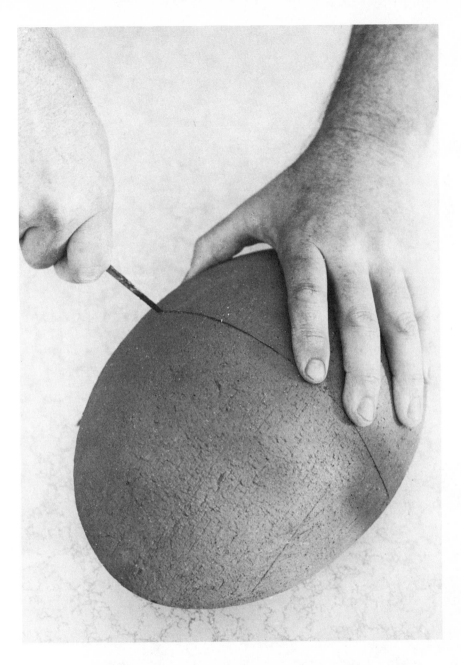

M-3 Cut the clay form in half (at right angles to the seam).

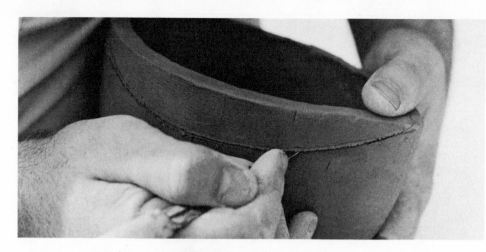

M-4. Cut a concave rim on each bowl form as shown with a knife, so that each half is shaped like a boat.

M-5. Cut a rectangular slab for the yoke. Place both halves upside-down on top of this slab, so that the bowls are lined up side by side. Push the clay of the rims of the bowls onto the slab, and reinforce the joint between the slab and the bowls with a coil (see **H-10,** p. 104). Notice that I am using a plastic bucket to support the slab as I work, so that the yoke curves slightly.

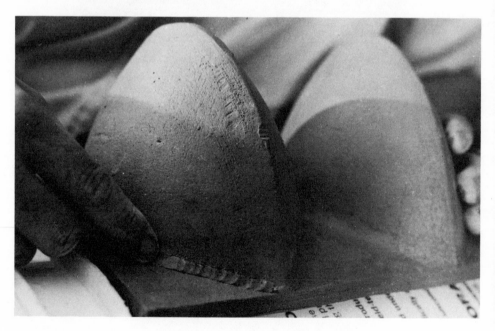

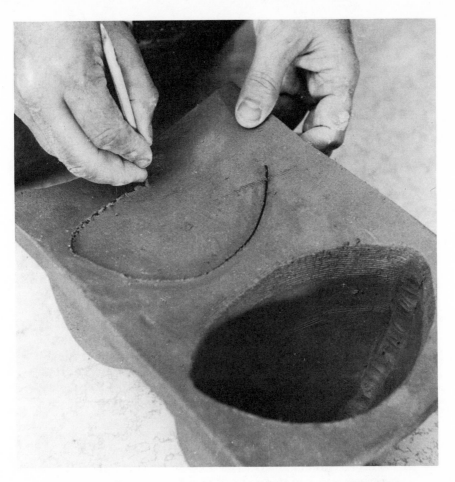

M-6. Cut out a top hole for each pot with a knife. With a coil, reinforce the joints inside the circumference of each pot. Clean the edges of the top holes with a hacksaw blade. To allow this planter to sit upright and not roll over, it is necessary to scrape the bottom of each pot with a hacksaw blade, to make a wide, flat base.

Let the planter dry and then fire it. Glaze the top slab and the inside of the pots, and fire again.

Variation: A variation of this technique can be used to make a dish garden, using one shallow elliptical shape made by the drape mold process. An example of this is shown on p. 189, in Raymond's description of how to plant a dish garden.

159

How To Use a Kiln

A kiln is an oven-like chamber that will bake, or fire, pottery to a hardened state. This makes its shape permanent, and transforms the clay so that it is impervious to moisture.

You will be firing each planter twice. Unfired pottery is called **green ware**. When the green ware has become thoroughly dry, it is placed in the kiln for the first firing. This is called **bisque firing** and pots that have already had this firing done are called **bisque ware**. At this stage the clay is hard enough to handle easily and is able to take a glaze.

The second firing is done after application of a glaze. This is called **glost** or **glaze firing** and pots that emerge from this second kiln stage are called **glazed ware**. The clay reaches a "mature" state, hardening completely, and the glaze fuses to the clay.

Pottery that is not going to be glazed at all should also undergo two firings (although this is not usually done in commercial productions). The two firings are more of a safety precaution in this case. If there is any excess water in the clay from insufficient drying, the pot might explode while being heated in the kiln. If a pot breaks during bisque firing, it will most likely only affect that one pot. The pieces that scatter will not harm the other pots in the kiln. However, if the preliminary bisque firing stage is skipped and you simply put green ware in the kiln with glazed ware that is undergoing a second firing, in the event of your pot shattering, its pieces might ruin the other glazed ware.

It takes a long time for a pot to be fired because the clay must be heated slowly and then slowly cooled. The first firing can take from 8-12 hours, and it may take as long for the pot to cool before you can remove it from the kiln. The second firing can take a couple of days, including the cooling period. Waiting for the kiln to cool can seem like waiting for Christmas!

Firing may seem to be a complicated business, but if you are using a kiln at a school or recreation center or any place where there are professionals or teachers in charge, you will most likely be renting kiln space and the firing will be done for you for a fee.

Drying Time Before Firing Time

Your pot should be "bone dry," that is, completely dry, before firing it. But how can you tell if your pot is dry enough to bisque-fire it?

The drying time is affected by many factors—whether the pot is dried inside or outside, the weather, humidity, temperature, draft, proximity to heat sources, etc. It may take anywhere from one day to one week to dry a pot thoroughly. There are two clues you can look for to decide

when your pot is sufficiently dry. First, if the clay is cold to the touch, it is too wet to fire. Second, as clay dries it will get lighter in color. The pot is completely dry when there are no darker areas on the clay indicating the presence of spots of moisture. Experience will teach you how to tell if your pot is ready for bisque firing.

Kiln Temperatures: Using Cones

Even if you are having your pots fired for you, you will find it interesting to know something about the details of the firing process. And for those who have their own kiln or plan to buy one, the following information should prove helpful.

If you are using earthenware clay you will probably be firing in a low-temperature kiln. If you are using stoneware clay, you will be using a high-temperature kiln (high-temperature kilns can also be adjusted to a lower temperature to accommodate earthenware clay).

A low-temperature kiln does not fire above 2000°F. (1,093°C.). I know this doesn't sound like a very low fire if you're used to baking bread! A high-temperature kiln will go up to 2,300°F. (1,260°C.) or higher.

How do you know how long to fire your pots? If you leave them in the kiln too long, they will eventually melt. Some kilns have an automatic shut-off system that closes down the heat once a certain temperature has been reached. If the kiln you are using does not have this feature, you will be able to use a device called a **cone** (sometimes referred to as a **pyrometric cone**).

Cones are long, thin objects made of ceramic materials that are designed to bend noticeably when the heat in the kiln reaches a predetermined temperature. You may purchase cones where you get your clay and other supplies.

Cones are used by placing them in the kiln in front of a peekhole in the kiln door or kiln wall. Different cones are made to bend at different temperatures. Check with your supplier to find out what cones you will need for the kind of clay and the kind of glaze you are using. The cones are numbered according to the temperatures at which they bend, starting from 022 (the lowest) and going through 01 and on to 12 (the highest temperature with which you will be concerned). See the table of cone temperatures in the Appendix, on p. 203.

The cone is placed upright on a stand at a certain angle (it should be pictured on the outside of the box of cones you buy). You can purchase a special cone stand, or make your own out of very moist clay mixed with about ⅓ sand or grog. Form a ball out of this clay and press the base of the cone into it. If you are using several different cones at one time, form a short clay coil and press the cones into the coil.

Bisque Firing

After your pot has become completely dry, it is ready for bisque firing. Many pots can be stacked closely together in the kiln because the clay will not stick during this firing.

You should bisque-fire earthenware and stoneware pots at cone 08, which is 1,733°F. (945°C.).

You must heat your kiln slowly the first several hours. There is water that remains in the clay even after thoroughly air-drying pottery. This water is chemically bound to the clay material itself, and requires heat of several hundred degrees to expel. This heating process must be done gradually to prevent the pottery from exploding due to excessive steam pressure in the clay.

During the first two hours of firing, I leave the kiln door open a crack to allow moisture to escape from the drying pottery.

After the kiln reaches its correct temperature for the bisque firing, turn off the heat. Allow the kiln to cool with the door closed until it reaches room temperature (usually about 8-12 hours). Then remove your bisque pottery. (If you are using your own kiln at home, consult the literature you receive from your kiln supplier for specific instructions applicable to your kiln).

Your pots are now hard and easy to handle so that you can apply a glaze if you wish.

Glost Firing

After glazing, place your pots into the kiln again. This time you must be sure that none of the glazed ware is touching the wall of the kiln or another pot. Glazed pots should be at least ½″ apart.

For stoneware, I use three cones. The first one is cone 8, which tells me the clay is about to reach the temperature at which it will mature (i.e., become permanently hardened). The second cone is cone 9 (2,282°F. or 1,250°C.) which tells me when to turn off the kiln. The third one is cone 10, which lets me know how much I might have overfired. The bending of each cone is the indicator that the particular stage has been reached.

The temperatures for glost-firing earthenware depend upon the particular clay and glaze purchased. Consult your supplier for the correct temperatures and cones to use.

After the kiln is shut off, allow it to cool (usually from 18-24 hours) and then remove your finished pots. If you remove pottery when it is too hot, the glaze may develop small, hairline cracks throughout the surface (this is known as "crazing" or "crackling").

Kiln Wash

To protect the kiln shelves from dripping glaze, I coat them with several layers of a wash made from equal parts of silica (200-mesh) and kaolin, a type of fine clay. You can purchase these at your ceramics supplier. Put on several thin coats of the wash until you accumulate a layer about 1/16″ thick. This makes your shelves easier to clean after glaze drips on them during the glost firing.

Buying Your Own Kiln

After your initiation into pottery making, you may want to consider buying your own kiln. The cost is not prohibitive. You can have a suitable electric kiln for no more than the price of a small portable TV set.

Of course the kiln you buy for home use may not be as large as the kiln you may use at a local school or studio. You can get a table-top kiln that is easy to move into place. Hook-up may require only a standard 110-volt outlet. Larger kilns usually require a 220-volt outlet, the kind an electric clothes dryer uses. The size of the outlet needed depends on the size of the kiln and the maximum temperature the kiln will reach.

You can buy either a high-fire or a low-fire kiln. A high-fire kiln will not cost very much more than a low-fire kiln, and will enable you to fire both earthenware and stoneware.

A gas kiln rather than an electric kiln is my own preference, because you can change the atmosphere to achieve a variety of results in your pottery. A gas kiln is probably too costly for the beginning home potter to consider. I would therefore recommend an electric kiln if you are going to buy one.

It would be difficult for me to instruct you on how to use your kiln. When the purchase is made, ask your dealer for the details of its operation since there are many kinds of kilns with different types of controls.

If you are exploring the possibility of buying a kiln, talk it over with your local ceramic supplier. Some suppliers are representatives of several kiln companies, and may suggest several kinds for you to consider.

You can also discuss the possibility of building your own kiln, which is not at all uncommon.

How To Mix and Apply Glazes

Mixing A Glaze

If you have purchased a dry glaze, add water to it and stir until it becomes liquid. Too much water will cause the glaze to be too thin. Glaze with too little water will cause it to be applied too thickly to your pottery. You will have to discover the proper "medium-gravy" consistency by trial and error.

You can test the thickness of the glaze by making some bisque-fired tiles ahead of time or using pot shards to dip into the mix as you add water. You will have the proper amount of water in the mix when the tile emerges after one dip with a glaze coat about as thick as a postcard. After you get a feeling for the right glaze consistency, it will not be necessary to repeat this test each time you mix a glaze.

After adding water to the glaze, pour it through a screen into a container, to break up any lumps in the mixture. Then mix it well. For a screen you can use anything from a tea strainer to a 200-mesh wire sieve. I recommend screening your glaze three times with a 60-80 mesh sieve. The finer the sieve, the more uniform the glaze will be in texture and color.

Applying a Glaze

Glaze should be applied to bisque-fired pots (pots that have been fired once).

Glaze 1. It is advisable to glaze the interior of the pot first. Pour the glaze into the pot.

Glaze 2. Pick up the pot and tilt it in a rotating manner, coating the interior completely while pouring the glaze out over the rim into another container.

Glaze 3. After the interior is dry, pour the glaze over the outside of the pot, resting the pot upside-down in a container. Try to do this quickly and in one flowing motion. You want to avoid repouring and overlapping as much as possible, because each pouring adds thickness to the glaze, and your goal is to apply an even coat.

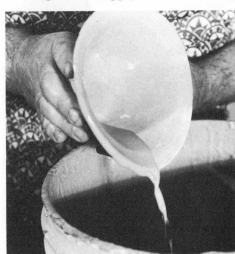

Glaze 4. If you have sufficient glaze prepared, you may dip the pot directly into the glaze instead of pouring it over the pot. This technique is best because it is easier to apply an even coat. If the pot has glaze on its base after dipping it in this fashion, remember to wipe it clean before you set it on the kiln shelf.

Some problems that might develop in glazing are:

Crackle — fine hairline cracking in the glaze after firing, usually when the pot is not cooled slowly enough. This can be considered either a decorative effect, or a defect (crazing).

Crawling — movement of glaze on the clay surface during the firing of a pot, leaving bare clay areas exposed. This usually happens from glazing over dusty pottery or applying a glaze too thickly.

Shivering — the flaking off of glaze from a glost-fired pot due to the use of an improper glaze. If this happens, another glaze should probably be tried.

Barnard Clay

If you decide not to glaze your planter, you may consider using Barnard Clay to stain a particular texture or to accent the linear patterns of a coil pot. I often choose this method myself.

Barnard Clay is a dark clay which will fuse to the pot when fired. The color is an attractive deep brown after firing.

Barnard Clay is applied only to stoneware; it is not suitable for earthenware.

Barnard 1. Mix the dry Barnard Clay with water to a smooth, thin, gravy-like consistency. Apply it liberally with a sponge.

Barnard 2. After it dries for a couple of minutes, wipe the pot with another sponge. This will leave the depressions in the pot's texture dark, and the top surfaces light. Now let the pot dry and fire it with the Barnard Clay stain the same as you would a glazed pot.

Part 3

Part 3

Houseplant Care

It's a good idea to live with your plant a while before making a pot for it. Study its shape and habits. The more you know and love your subject, the more fitting your container will be.

Also think about where your plant will be growing. Try to visualize the pot and plant as it will look in a particular place in a room, so that the plant you choose and the pot you make will blend in with its surroundings.

SUPPLIES

All kinds of supplies for the pot and plant enthusiast can be found in garden shops. These include potting soils and potting mixes, insecticides, fungicides, plant foods, and books on plant care and culture. Encourage the dealers you visit to stock the clay and other materials you need for making your own planters. Also, when you frequent these shops, notice the styles of the pots on display for inspiration in designing your own planters.

Potting Mixes

You may now be using prepared potting mixes with which you are satisfied, or you may wish to make potting mixes yourself. Some of the ingredients used in potting mixes are: perlite, vermiculite, wood chips, shredded peat moss, tree bark, sand, gravel, worm castings and charcoal.

Water retention is the main characteristic of perlite, vermiculite, wood chips, peat moss and bark. Perlite also keeps the soil well aerated. Sand and gravel allow space for aeration with some presence of moisture. Worm castings

173

make a rich additive, providing good nutrients to the soil. Charcoal has the unique function of giving "sweetness" to a potting mix by absorbing sulfides and releasing carbonates.

Here are my recipes for three good potting mixes:

1. Use perlite, peat moss and vermiculite in equal amounts. Add enough water to moisten, but not to saturate.

2. Combine sand, wood chips and peat moss in equal amounts.

3. Mix together one half worm castings, one fourth wood chips or bark, and one fourth peat moss.

After you have tried these combinations, you will notice that these mixes are ideal because not only do the textures bind together, but they also break apart easily. They are all "fast" mixes which will not waterlog unless you grossly overwater them in a pot with no drainage hole. Remember that the function of a good potting soil is to let water in, and let water out.

For potting in containers without drainholes:

Use equal parts of charcoal and gravel to fill the bottom ¼ of the pot. Then put one of the above "fast" mixes on top.

Bridwell Sleeve

The Bridwell Sleeve is a device that I developed to plant in a container without a drainhole, or in a very tall and narrow-necked pot in which it would be hard to fit your plant without damaging the roots. The supplies needed for the Bridwell sleeve are nylon stockings, soft black wire, some stiff wire, green sphagnum moss, and 1-inch mesh chickenwire. See the photo sequence on p. 178 for an illustration of how to make the Bridwell Sleeve.

Plant Foods

Plant feeding programs are indispensable if you want to cultivate healthy houseplants. Choose any one of the prepared plant foods you can find in a garden shop and follow the directions on the label precisely; the manufacturer isn't just putting that on to entertain you, he's putting it on there to help you.

In most cases to feed a plant sufficiently you should feed it every second or third watering. Some people feed every time they water, and they are quite successful with this. I think we have to see what technique works best for individual plants.

Leaf Wash

On a regular program, visit your plants and remove all dead, diseased or disfigured leaves. Your plants are continually growing subjects and need to have these old leaves removed before they decay or culture disease.

This is also a good time to use leaf wash to clean the foliage. Leaf wash is essential to remove dust, grease and hydrocarbons that might clog the leaf's pores through which transpiration takes place. Plain water does not have the solvent necessary to do this effectively. You can buy a commercial leaf wash preparation in your garden shop. If leaf wash is not available, place a pinch of Epsom salt in a quart of water and use this solution in a spray dispenser. **Do not use this mixture on African Violets.**

SPECIAL POTTING INSTRUCTIONS

I will discuss how to pot your plants for these projects selected from those presented in Part 2:

1. Paddle and Scoop Planter with Cacti and Succulents (p. 176).
2. Pinch Planter with Herbs (p. 176).
3. Coil Planter with Asparagus Fern (p. 177).
4. Slab Box Planter with Cobra-Leaf Plectranthus (p. 178).
5. Open Coil Planter with Melon Peperomia (p. 186).
6. Dish Garden with Sedum and Scotch Moss (p. 189).

Paddle and Scoop Planter with Cacti and Succulents

Use the "cram" technique for cacti and succulents planted in this pot. Hold the cactus in place in the pot with a pair of tongs. Add some coarse, moist mix (gravel and charcoal add to all-purpose soil mix), and then cram additional potting mix between the cactus root and pot wall with a stick or putty knife.

For the succulents, keep a fair amount of soil with the plant's roots, and place the plant in the pot. Then cram additional soil around it in the same manner as above

Pinch Planter with Herbs

a-1. These herbs are very easy to pot. Cover the drainage holes with broken pieces of pot. Use one of the fast potting mixes described in the section on Supplies, p. 173, and install the plants. We are using parsley, upland cress, and thyme—cne variety in each section of the pot.

a-2. Use sharp clippers to clean away any unsightly leaves, and later to harvest the growth of these plants for perking up sauces, salads, etc. Begin feeding these herbs immediately with a water soluble plant food and you will be surprised at how frequently you can harvest them.

Coil Planter with Asparagus Fern

This coil planter is an easy pot to work with because it has a drainhole. Simply place a piece of broken pot over the hole. Use an all-purpose mix, or any on of the three-ingredient potting mixes described on p. 174. Partially fill the planter with this potting soil. Set the plant in place, and finish by adding potting soil almost to the rim of the planter. Press the soil firmly between the rootball of the fern and the wall of the planter, using your fingers extended in a rigid motion.

Slab Box Planter with Cobra-Leaf Plectranthus

This is a tall planter without a drainhole and with a narrow-necked opening. It is a good example to demonstrate the use of the **Bridwell Sleeve,** a device that will aid in potting this Cobra-Leaf Plectranthus, or any other plant, into a similar pot.

You will need a nylon stocking, soft black wire, some stiff wire, green sphagnum moss, and 1-inch mesh chickenwire (available at a building supply store).

Before beginning, soak the green moss in water from 15 to 20 minutes and squeeze it out so that it is still moist. Then follow the illustrated directions below.

b-1. I am preparing this plant to be inserted into the 5-inch opening at the top of its container. The diameter of the plant's rootball is 6¼″. The rootball is placed firmly on an inverted pot to prevent the rootball from breaking away too rapidly as I trim it. With a slim, sharp spatula, I am repeatedly slicing off layers of soil about ¼″ thick with each stroke, until the ball size is reduced to approximately 4″ in diameter.

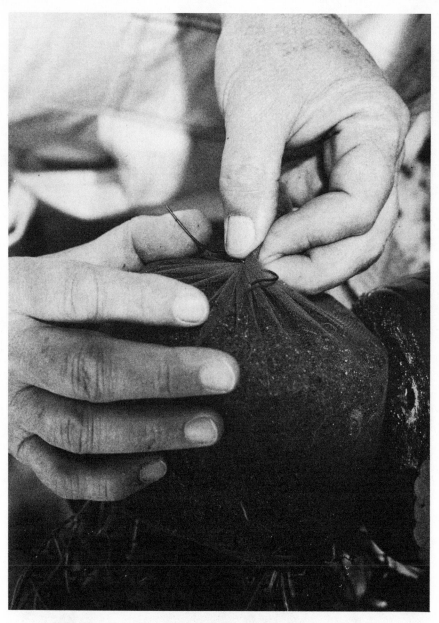

b-2. Sheathe the rootball with a piece of nylon stocking. The stocking will help retain the fine soil around the rootball. Then tie the stocking closed with soft black wire.

b-3. Cut a piece of 1-inch mesh chickenwire about 14"
square (or to fit your plant). Pat a thin layer of green moss
over the surface of the chickenwire.

b-4. Place the sheathed rootball on the moss-lined wire retainer.

b-5. Attach a 10- or 12-inch length of soft black wire to the chickenwire mesh at one side. Run the wire through the mesh at the other side, using this for a closing suture to bind the two ends of the mesh together.

b-6. Cut the chickenwire that extends down past the rootball into four segments. Press the segments closed so that they encase the bottom of the rootball, and secure with soft black wire.

b-7. Twist all of the wires tightly closed. The wire ends you cannot bury safely into the moss should be clipped off closely with a wire cutter.

b-8. Shape a sling of stiff wire to wrap around the entire rootball of the plant. Make loops on each end of the wire (to use as fingerholds), bend the wire around the rootball, and secure it to the mesh with small clips of soft wire.

Dip entire sleeve portion of the plant into a container of water for two or three minutes. This will give it a thorough watering sufficient to last several days. Then with your fingers in the wire fingerholds, insert the plant into the pot as shown. The fingerhold loops rest on the rim of the pot. This makes the plant removable.

Open Coil Planter with Melon Peperomia

The open structure of this planter requires the use of green sphagnum moss to keep soil and water from leaking out. The following illustrated sequence will show you how to plant a Melon Peperomia in this type of pot.

c-1. This is green sphagnum moss, available at any houseplant shop or nursery. Remove the moss from its package, soak it in water for 15 to 20 minutes, squeeze out excess water and it is ready to use. There is no mesh lining to this bowl. The moss is neatly arranged directly in the bowl, patted down flat, and firmly pressed into the sides (try to push the moss through the openings).

c-2. After this bowl is lined with moss, use a strong pick to pull and tease the moss through the openings to help it stay in place.

c-3. Start lining the moss layer with a three-part potting mix of your choice, as described on p. 174, or use a prepared potting soil. The mix shown here is made from equal parts of peat moss, vermiculite, and perlite. Simply place about a half-inch soil lining inside the moss liner.

c-4. We are placing two Melon Peperomia of the 3-inch size into dibbles (impressions) made in the potting soil, and pinch-trimming the rootballs to help insert them firmly in the planter.

After potting is completed, this plant can be easily watered by dipping the entire bowl in a sinkful of water. Then rest it on the drainboard at an angle, to allow the water to drain.

Variation of Drape Mold

Dish Garden with Sedum and Scotch Moss

This dish garden is a variation of the drape mold used for the double planter. It is made from a single shallow bowl. The elliptical shape shows so much strength in supporting margins of the garden, and yet has such a graceful, flowing line. The dish garden gives me the opportunity to combine natural stone with foliage in a miniature setting. It is not obtrusive in size for placement on a table.

d-1. This beautifully-shaped pot could as quickly be used as a "catch-all" tray on a desk, but we will use it here for a dish garden. Spread a bottom layer of coarse charcoal and pea gravel in the dish.

d-2. Add a layer of all-purpose mix (you can use one of those on p. 174). Trim the Scotch Moss to fit the scale of the dish, by turning the moss upside-down in your hand and cutting through the rootball.

d-3. Place Scotch Moss in the dish and arrange the potting soil for a space to add the Sedum (a type of succulent).

d-4. Remove the Sedum from its tray, and break it into small ball sections. Press them into position in the dish, filling in with small amounts of mix as the planting progresses.

d-5. After brushing away the debris from planting, add small stones in subtle, natural-looking positions.

HINTS ON PRUNING

In addition to general information about pruning, I will talk about how to prune these specific plants selected from those presented in Part 2:

1. Hanging Coil Planter with Wandering Jew (p. 195).

2. Spherical Mold Planter with Swedish Ivy and Wandering Jew (p. 196).

3. Hanging Hemisphere Planter with Plectranthus Africanus (p. 197).

4. High-Footed Bowl Planter with Spider Plant (p. 198).

5. Lamp Planter with Asparagus Fern and Wandering Jew (p. 198).

6. Dish Garden with Scotch Moss and Sedum (p. 199).

When and Why To Prune

Some people feel shy about pruning their plants, as though each cut of a stem were some unnatural desecration. Now, I certainly believe in kindness to plants, just as I believe in kindness to children and animals. But we all admit there should be some training going on, some pattern of discipline to give our children the opportunity to be socially acceptable and desirable. I am not trying to sell you on the idea that plants have personalities, but only on the idea that we can give plants shape and style to make them more or less aesthetically desirable. This is the type of discipline that we should feel free to exercise on plants.

For example, you may have houseplants that have become too long and scraggly. Pruning will reduce your plant to a more pleasing size. And through the technique of pinching, which I'll explain a little later on, you will also be able to encourage a more bushy growth of leaves.

Keep in mind that since you have spent so much time creating a unique pot for your plant, you don't want to let the plant expand to the point of entirely covering up the pot. The plant can get out of proportion to its container without proper care. You can extablish a beautiful relationship again between pot and plant by careful pruning.

Pruning is not only aesthetically pleasing, it's also healthy for your plants. Pruning encourages more vigorous growth. After a plant is pruned, it has a greater proportion of roots in relation to the amount of foliage. With less foliage to feed, the roots have more energy to spare and can direct that energy to generate new foliage.

Get Rid of Dead Leaves

You must cultivate the practice of removing discolored leaves as well as old and dying leaves. Seeing disfigured leaves on a plant reminds me of a beautiful woman smiling at you with nice polished ivory teeth, and she's just eaten a salad and there's a little bit of spinach left on one tooth! It shatters the image. So any time I have a brown leaf among the green foliage, I simply clip away the off-color foliage (or brush the spinach off the tooth, as it were). I know we aren't supposed to do this for each other, but it certainly looks better.

You also want to clip off dying leaves to prevent decay and disease from setting in. When you pick off such a leaf, this is a good time to inspect it to make sure that the plant doesn't have aphids or some other insect attacking it. The time to act is when you've got just one or two leaves infested, instead of later when the whole plant may be affected

Pruning Gives You a Bonus: A New Plant

A bonus that you get from pruning your plants is the beginning of a whole new baby plant. Taking stems that you have clipped and starting new plants from them is a method of propagation that beats going to the plant shop every time you want a new plant. You simply have to put the clipped stem in water until it develops roots, and then plant this new growth in another pot.

To sum up what I've said, regular pruning: a) reshapes your plant; b) puts the plant back into proportion with its pot; c) promotes more vigorous growth, and; e) gives you starters for new plants.

When To Throw Out a Plant

I'd like to add a word here about something quite a bit more drastic than pruning — throwing out dead plants. You should remember that plants aren't made in machine shops. They are God's creations and they grow and there are certain things we can do for them, but they don't stay alive and healthy forever. If I have a plant which I've been feeding carefuly, insecticiding carefully, and for some reason it dies, I accept this fact and realize that it is dead and that now it is just garbage. Therefore I get rid of it. I could have ten beautiful plants and one poor looking one and someone coming in would notice only the one poor looking one. They would wonder what's wrong with me that I can't bring plants back from the dead. Well, no one can do that.

Although you may feel it is crass to unceremoniously dump a plant that's been with you for two or three years, you have to take the same attitude that you have when throwing away lettuce leaves left over from a salad, or when you vigorously twist off the tops of carrots and throw them in the garbage. A dead plant is just that and we have to learn to deal with loss and failure.

Look at it from a very positive viewpoint. When a plant of mine dies, I clean out the pot, wash it carefully, and let it have sun or at least air exposure for a couple of weeks before I plant in it again. In dealing with plants, I always have a new one coming in which I'd like to try in that particular pot.

Pruning Techniques

Let's get back to thinking about your living, growing plants. I'm going to talk about a few of the plants that we potted in the containers Roger made for them and describe to you what goes through my mind when I look them over for pruning.

Pruning is partly a matter of taste and style. When you let your plant grow to a greater density than when you first potted it, you see less of the container and the pot now becomes an accent to the suggestions of the plant. There are other times that you want the pot to appear more bold, and you can accomplish that by pruning.

The way to reduce a plant to its original size and shape is to clip the long stems or runners. The place to do this is above the leaf node. A leaf node is the joint where a leaf is attached to the stem. Of course there are as many nodes on a stem as there are leaves. A good rule of thumb to follow in deciding at what junctures to cut is to remember that in order to retain the natural beauty of the plant, the clipped stems should be of different lengths. That means you want to cut each stem at a node that is a different distance from the plant crown (the crown is where the foliage begins at the bottom of the plant, just above the roots and soil).

It's a good idea to extend the pruning and shaping process over a 3- or 4-week period. This way, your plant never looks as if it were hard-shorn. You won't miss a piece at a time if you prune slowly instead of in one radical move.

You may have a hanging planter and you would like to cut back on the foliage to bring the pot to the foreground. Then you could just shear around this plant, taking off everything longer than 8-12 inches. When you are ready to hang the pot again, you will be able to see the planter with all of its profusion of color and foliage adorning the top.

Here are specific examples of pruning techniques used in some of the Pots & Plants projects we present in this book.

Hanging Coil Planter with Wandering Jew

In the large sunroom at our home, we now have the hanging coil planter with the Wandering Jew, the one called

Zebrina, rather than Piggyback as on Page 76. This plant has a beautiful reddish-violet color with green variations, and with very long branches cascading down from the brim of the pot. This planting provides a very attractive alternative to the Piggyback planting shown earlier in the book.

In its present situation here in the sunroom, the planter has a perch on the table and more foliage has been added to the crown of the plant. We did this by cutting some runners from the plant, putting them in a jar of water, waiting for them to form roots, and installing them in the soil with the rest of the plant when the shoots were 3-5 inches high.

The new shoots really seem to love it in there and the whole appearance of the pot has changed. It is a mass of foliage up at the top of the pot, and there are still many runners hanging down. Because the plant is on the table, these runners turn up toward the light, and you can see what is really a rejuvenation of growth. The pruning has stimulated these runners to grow.

This is one of the great benefits of being able to topwork plants—you are really involved with new growth most of the time.

Pruning produced a new style for this Zebrina, a very lovely shape. It is for this very same reason that we go to beauty shops to have our hair styled in different ways. Just as we make cosmetic changes in our hair, so we make cosmetic changes in our plants.

Spherical Mold Planter
with Swedish Ivy and Wandering Jew

Here is an example of "forced pruning." I was transporting this pot (shown on p. 120) from Roger's place to my place. I was intending to be very careful with it to keep it in good condition for him.

In backing my car, however, I bumped a telephone pole and the pot rolled around in the trunk of the car. When I got home I found that the edge of the pot had worked just like a die cutter, breaking off many branches of the Swedish Ivy. The Swedish Ivy originally had at least three branches on it with 8-9 inches of longitudinal growth, and then it got sheared back 3-4 inches.

But you know, all is not lost—the plant is coming back beautifully. So this plant has become a very good example of how pruning, even unintentional pruning, can result in very vigorous growth. The roots were given the chance to divert their energy from maintaining the existing foliage to promoting new growth once the old foliage was cut back.

Hanging Hemisphere Planter with Plectranthus Africanus

This Plectranthus is the one with the beautiful lateral branching (p. 135), and I can see there's a little care that I want to give it. I see a branch, about 6 inches long, that I'm very interested in because I'd like to take this branch off and root it in water. Plectranthus will water-root very nicely, as a rule.

Plectranthus is part of the mint family, and you may have noticed on other mints that there is a characteristic square stem that can look very coarse and rugged, almost like a beam for a building. That's what this branch looks like. I'll cut it off where it's joined to the root crown, next to the main stem.

This branch has internodes about 1 inch long. The node of a plant is where the leaf attaches to the main stem, and the internode is the distance between nodes, or between leaves on a stem. I'm going to take the leaves off at the bottom two nodes so that I have two inches of bare stem at the bottom, enough to put the stem in water to root it.

After the stem has rooted, I will plant it in a pot, and pinch the growing tips of the plant to see how much side-branching I can get. The pinching technique is simply the nipping off of an end of a stem or runner with your thumb and forefinger so that two branches grow out from one stem (sidebranching). This results in a fuller, more bushy plant and can be done to change the shape of any plant that looks too scrawny. Sidebranching is quite a wondrous thing, and gives you another means of influencing your plant's appearance.

There are two methods of pinching. The hard-pinch, or hard shear, is the cutting of a stem far back near the crown of the plant. The soft pinch is the cutting of a stem at its growing tip.

High-Footed Bowl Planter with Spider Plant

Spider plants (Chlorophytum) are very prolific. They usually have long, arching leaves that go out from the crown, and from these many little plantlets form so that the main plant is surrounded by miniatures hanging all around.

I admit that for a hanging pot or basket, a cascade of these plantlets is very beautiful and a sight to behold. But in this particular case (pictured on p. 136), I wanted to create a balanced symmetry with just the main part of the Chlorophytum.

I didn't have a plant in stock for this pot, so I bought a new one and removed all those plantlets or bract-growths. The results, as you can see, is a nicely shaped Chlorophytum without any outriggers hanging down.

These bracts root very readily, either in a sand medium or in water.

Lamp Planter with Asparagus Fern and Wandering Jew

The lamp planter (seen on p. 140) is an example of companion planting done with Zebrina-Wandering Jew and the Asparagus sprengeri Fern. We haven't done any pruning of the fern before, we have just let it grow and I don't know how many weeks it will be before I'll do some selective pruning on it. I am making a mental picture of how it looks at this point, because it is so graceful that each time I prune it, I'll want to be able to prune it back to just where it is now. That means that I won't give it a haircut like the bowl over the little boy's head. But I will discriminatingly take out alternate branches, or every third or fourth branch that seems to be long. I will clip that branch clear back to the crown of the plant and let new growth form.

You will notice, by the way, that the new little shoots that pop up out of the soil look more like a spindly kind of asparagus than a fern when they first come out. They have no leafiness on them at all, and only as they mature do they take on the characteristics of the regular fern.

On the Zebrina that the fern is co-planted with, there was one branch that didn't have enough side-growth, so we did a pinch on it. We took off the first two leaves on the tip of the runner, and now it is sidebranching beautifully.

Dish Garden with Scotch Moss and Sedum

The dish garden I'd like to discuss here is the one I illustrated under planting techniques (p. 189). I've done some work on pruning it so that it stays in proportion to the small pot it's in.

Scotch moss looks like a field of grass so profuse that you'd worry about a brush fire. You can just use a barbering technique on it, and trim it clear back to the base growth. It comes back again profusely, just like hair on a baby's head.

Sedum is a minute, broad-leafed plant, and it was pruned back too. It was not a gross shearing though, in the way I cut the Scotch moss. This was a discriminate cutting of the long pieces back to the leaf joint. In most cases, these branches where I cut back have one or more new branches growing out from that junction.

I guess people are always manicuring their nails, or doing something fidgety which would really drive this little plant out of its mind. But here we are manicuring the plant to keep it the perfect size for its container, the small dish garden.

Appendix

CERAMIC SUPPLIERS

Note: This is by no means an exhaustive list. Consult your Yellow Pages for dealers close to you.

California

Aardvark
1400 E. Pomona
Santa Ana, Ca. 92705

Leslie Ceramics Supply Co.
1212 San Pablo Avenue
Berkeley, Ca. 94706

Western Ceramics Supply Co.
1601 Howard Street
San Francisco, Ca. 94103

Westwood Ceramic Supply Co.
14400 Lomitas Avenue
City of Industry, Ca. 91744

Florida

Bennett Pottery Supply, Inc.
10520 S.W. 184th Terrace
Miami, Fl. 33157

Potters World
4930 Distribution Drive
Tampa, Fl. 33619

Illinois

The Clay People
3345 North Halsted
Chicago, Ill. 60657

Robbins Clay
1021 W. Lill
Chicago, Ill. 60614

Indiana

Amaco-American Art
   Clay Co., Inc.
4717 W. 16th Street
Indianapolis, Ind. 46222

Kentucky

Owl Creek Pottery
11416 Shelbyville Road
Louisville, Ky. 40243

Maryland

Eagle Ceramics, Inc.
12264 Wilkins Avenue
Rockville, Md. 20852

Massachusetts

Rare Earth Mudworks, Inc.
70 Merrimac Street Creek
Amesbury, Mass. 01913

Michigan

Rovin Ceramics
6912 Shaefer Road
Dearborn, Mi. 48126

Minnesota

Minnesota Clay
8001 Grand Avenue So.
Bloomington, Minn. 55420

Paramount Ceramic, Inc.
220 No. State
Fairmont, Minn 56031

Missouri

Good Earth Clays, Inc.
3054 South West Blvd.
Kansas City, Mo. 64108

New Jersey

Byrne Ceramic Supply Co., Inc.
95 Bartley Road
Flanders, N.J. 07836

Creek-Turn Ceramic Supply
Route 38
Hainesport, N.J. 08036

Standard Clay Mines
Camp Meeting Avenue
Skillman, N.J. 08558

Stewart Clay Co., Inc.
P. O. Box 18
400 Jersey Avenue

New Mexico

Anhowe Ceramic Supply, Inc.
3825 Commercial St., N. E.
Albuquerque, N.M. 87107

New York

Baldwin Pottery
540 La Guardia Place
New York, N.Y. 10012

Firehouse Ceramics
238 Mulberry Street
New York, N.Y. 10012

Miller Ceramics, Inc.
8934 N. Seneca Street
Weedsport, N.Y. 13166

Pennsylvania

Arch T. Flower Co.
Queen St. & Ivy Hill Rd.
Philadelphia, Pa. 19118

The Clay Pot
104 Wagner Drive
Bethel Park, Pa. 15102

Potlatch Pottery
722 West Erie Avenue
Philadelphia, Pa. 19140

Washington

Westby Ceramic Supply /
  Mfg. Co.
620 N. 85th Street
Seattle, Wa. 98103

TABLE OF KILN TEMPERATURES

Cones (sometimes called pyrometric cones) measure the effect of heat on the pottery inside a kiln. They are numbered starting with 022 and going up to 42, but for the planters in this book you need only be concerned with cones up to number 12. A table showing the relationship between cone number and temperature is printed below. Keep in mind, though, that this is only an approximate relationship, since cones do not measure actual degrees but rather the heat at work as it affects the clay material of your pot. Fahrenheit and Centigrade (Celsius) degrees are both indicated.

Cone No.	Degrees F.	Degrees C.	Cone No.	Degrees F.	Degrees C.
022	1085°	585°	05	1886°	1030°
021	1103°	595°	04	1922°	1050°
020	1157°	625°	03	1976°	1080°
019	1166°	630°	02	2003°	1095°
018	1238°	670°	01	2030°	1110°
017	1328°	720°	1	2057°	1125°
016	1355°	735°	2	2075°	1135°
015	1418°	770°	3	2093°	1145°
014	1463°	795°	4	2129°	1165°
013	1517°	825°	5	2156°	1180°
012	1544°	840°	6	2174°	1190°
011	1607°	875°	7	2210°	1210°
010	1634°	890°	8	2237°	1225°
09	1706°	930°	9	2282°	1250°
08	1733°	945°	10	2300°	1260°
07	1787°	975°	11	2345°	1285°
06	1841°	1005°	12	2390°	1310°

GLAZE FORMULAS

If you choose to mix your own glazes you can find formulas in many ceramic books. I will pass on to you a few glazes which appeal to me and are dependable at cone 9 (see the table of cone temperatures, p. 201). I often add 2 percent bentonite to a glaze;   this makes the glazed ware easier to handle before firing.

Opaque, White, Semi-Mat
Potash Feldspar	49 gm
Kaolin	20 gm
Whiting	4 gm
Dolomite	19 gm
Tin Oxide	8 gm
	100 gm

Dark Bluish Purple
Potash Feldspar	53.7 gm
Whiting	12.9 gm
Colemanite	2.5 gm
Kaolin	6.0 gm
Flint	22.4 gm
Zinc Oxide	2.5 gm
	100.0 gm

+ Black Iron Oxide   3.0 gm
+ Rutile   3.0 gm

Medium Blue
Potash Feldspar	39.0 gm
Potash Feldspar	39.0 gm
Whiting	21.5 gm
Kaolin	20.2 gm
Flint	15.2 gm
Titanium Oxide	4.1 gm
	100.0 gm

+ Cobalt Carbonate   1.5 gm

Iron Red Plum
Potash Feldspar	25 gm
Whiting	25 gm
Kaolin	20 gm
Flint	30 gm
	100 gm

+ Red Iron Oxide   15 gm

Glossy Yellow with Brown
Dolomite	15 gm
Cornwall Stone	40 gm
Whiting	10 gm
Kaolin	25 gm
Flint	10 gm
	100.0 gm

+ Rutile   5 gm
+ Red Iron Oxide   3 gm

Celedon
Potash Feldspar	36.5 gm
Whiting	18.2 gm
Kaolin	25 gm
Flint	27.2 gm
Dolomite	4.5 gm
	100.0 gm

+ Yellow Ochre   4.0 gm

GLOSSARY OF CERAMIC TERMS

Barnard Clay. A type of dark stain that can be used on stoneware instead of a glaze.

Bats. Boards on which pots can rest while being worked on or while drying.

Bisque. Pottery that has already been fired once and is ready for glazing. Except in commercial productions, this is ordinarily the first stage before the final firing.

Body. A mix of clay ingredients used for pottery making, as in earthenware body or stoneware body.

Casting Plaster. A type of plaster that can be purchased as a dry powder to be mixed with water. Used for making molds.

Clay. Fine particles of material extracted from the earth's crust; when water is added to it, the material can be manipulated into a particular shape without cracking.

Coils. Rope-like pieces of clay used to build pottery.

Cones. Long, thin ceramic objects that indicate the temperature pottery has reached inside a kiln, by bending at a predetermined level of heat.

Cone Mold. A hollow form placed on the inside of a pot to support and shape the clay during construction.

Crackle. Fine hairline cracking in the glaze of a pot after firing. This can be considered either a defect (crazing) or a decorative effect.

Crawling. Movement of glaze on the clay during firing, leaving bare areas of clay unintentionally exposed. This usually happens from glazing over dusty pottery or applying a glaze too thickly.

Drape Mold. A hollow form into which a slab of clay is draped; the slab will assume the shape of the mold.

Earthenware Body. A type of clay used for pottery making that is fired at relatively low temperatures (less than 2000°F. or 1093°C.). It is the most common type of clay available, and is used widely in the ceramics industry for a variety of objects, from art ware to sewer pipe.

Filler. Sand or grog (see below) added to clay to inhibit cracking and warping.

Foot. The base of a pot.

Glost. The second or final firing of pottery, done after application of a glaze. The raw glaze will become a hard glassy coating at this firing, and unglazed clay will harden into its final state.

Green Ware. Unfired pottery.

Grog. A material made of fired and ground up clay, added to pottery clay as a filler to reduce the chances of pottery shrinkage and warping. Sand is another material used for this same purpose.

Handbuilding. The technique of making pots without a potter's wheel.

Kneading. The process of manipulating clay by hand to eliminate air pockets and make it into a homogeneous mass.

Leather-hard. The state that clay reaches when it is stiff, yet still moist (it won't easily change shape in handling). This is an ideal state for carving or other finish work to be done to the clay

Mat. A non-glossy finish characteristic of certain glazes.

Maturity. The state that a clay pot or a glazed pot reaches when it has been fired to the heat required for final hardening. The temperature needed to reach this state is called the maturation temperature.

Mesh. The number of spaces per inch in a screen; the higher the mesh number, the finer the particles sifted through it.

Metalic Oxide. The chemical name for a type of stain used on pottery, also the coloring ingredient in a glaze, as in iron oxide.

Mold. A hollow form into which you can put soft pieces of clay, the clay will harden to the shape of the mold.

Paddling. The process of using a stick to firmly tap clay in order to shape it, also used to modify the surface texture clay.

Pinching. The technique of shaping clay into pots by using the thumb and forefinger.

Plaster Wheel. A cylinder made out of plaster that is rolled across the clay to impress designs (stamping tool).

Plasticity. The quality of clay that allows its formation into various shapes without cracking.

Shivering. The flaking off of glaze from a glost-fired pot due to an improper combination of glaze and clay.

Slab. A ⅜" thick, flat mass of clay from which different shapes can be cut to construct pottery.

Slip. A loose mixture of clay with a liberal amount of water, applied with a brush at the juncture of two clay pieces to help them stick together.

Stamping. The technique of pressing an object onto a slab of clay to create a texture or design.

Stoneware Body. A clay used for pottery making that requires a relatively high temperature to mature.

Wedging. The process of cutting and pressing together masses of clay to remove air pockets and make the clay homogenous (it serves the same function as kneading).

GLOSSARY OF HOUSE PLANT TERMS

Bract-Growth. A tiny plantlet that forms at the end of the stems of a spider plant, this can be taken off and used to propagate a new plant.

Bridwell Sleeve. A device to aid in potting plants, made out of moss, wire and nylon stocking.

Companion Planting. The potting of two or more varieties of plants in one container.

Crown. The part of a plant above the roots at which foliage begins.

Dish Garden. A shallow pot or dish planted with several plants and ornamental pebbles to form a miniature garden.

Fast Mix. A soil mixture for potting composed of a combination of organic and inert ingredients (lised in the section on Potting).

Internode. The space between two leaves that are attached to a stem.

Leaf Node. The juncture at which a leaf is joined to a stem.

Leaf Wash. A liquid preparation that contains a solvent to remove particles from the leaves that might clog the leaf pores.

Pinching. The technique of clipping off a stem with thumb and forefinger to encourage the growth of two branches from one stem.

Pruning. Cutting leaves and/or stems from a plant to shape it and encourage new growth.

Rootball. The entire clump of roots of a plant.

Sidebranching. The growth of two branches from one stem after pinching (see above).

Water-root. A method of propagation by which a clipping taken from a plant is placed in water until roots form and the new plant can be potted.